TEACHER GUIDE FOR

APRIL RAINTREE AND IN SEARCH OF APRIL RAINTREE

A Trauma-Informed Approach to Teaching
Stories of Indigenous Survivance, Family Separation,
and the Child Welfare System

CHRISTINE M'LOT
With **DR. KARLEE D. FELLNER**

PORTAGE & MAIN PRESS

ISBN 978-1-77492-094-7

Portage & Main Press gratefully acknowledges the financial support of the Government of Canada as well as the Province of Manitoba through the Department of Sport, Culture, Heritage and Tourism and the Manitoba Book Publishing Tax Credit for our publishing activities.

Funded by the Government of Canada
Financé par le gouvernement du Canada | Canada

Printed and bound in Canada by Rapido Books
Design by Jennifer Lum

To the students and teachers who have embraced the pages of "April Raintree" with open hearts, recognizing its profound educational value for all learners. May this guide serve as a compass on your journey to explore the rich tapestry of Indigenous experiences and the resilience of the human spirit. In the face of unimaginable suffering, the story of April Raintree and her sister Cheryl reminds us that even amidst adversity, one can still forge a path towards a good life. It is a testament to the enduring survivance of Indigenous communities and the power of hope.

—CM

to my son, Naatósíniipi.
to all of our ancestors and relatives who have kept
our cultures, languages, and teachings alive.
to the future generations who will carry
our cultures, languages, and teachings forward.
ay ay

—KF

Also issued in electronic format: ISBN 978-1-77492-096-1 (PDF)

27 26 25 24   1 2 3 4 5

PORTAGE & MAIN PRESS
www.portageandmainpress.com
Winnipeg, Manitoba
Treaty 1 Territory and homeland of the Métis Nation

TABLE OF CONTENTS

INTRODUCTION

USING THIS GUIDE

This guide supports teachers in creating dynamic learning experiences for their students and maintaining a respectful and dignified approach to Indigenous topics while studying the novels *April Raintree* and *In Search of April Raintree*.

April Raintree and *In Search of April Raintree* are most appropriate for grades 9 to 12, as the story deals with difficult topics including child welfare apprehensions, bullying, racism, addictions, sexual assault, and suicide.

The activities suggested in this guide are appropriate for English Language Arts; Social Studies; History; Current Topics in First Nations, Métis, and Inuit Studies; and Global Issues: Citizenship and Sustainability. Some are also relevant to the Arts Education, Psychology, Physical Education/Health Education, Mathematics, and Science curricula in many regions. A number of these activities encourage cross-curricular connections and collaborations with other teachers.

April Raintree is the youth-friendly version of *In Search of April Raintree. In Search of April Raintree* includes a detailed scene involving sexual assault that has been purposely left out of *April Raintree* to give educators the option of teaching this important novel without vivid descriptions of the assault.

This teacher guide for *April Raintree* and *In Search of April Raintree* offers several significant benefits for grade 9 to 12 students. With its focus on educational activities promoting wellness, improving literacy, and fostering inquiry, the guide provides a structured framework for educators to explore the narratives and broader themes of Indigenous identity, cultural heritage, racism, foster care, and the legacy of colonialism. This holistic approach helps students grasp the deeper socio-cultural and historical context surrounding the story, furthering a comprehensive understanding of these themes and their impact on wellness. Moreover, the guide incorporates discussions and activities that encourage students to reflect on the characters' emotional and psychological well-being, fostering empathy and awareness of the importance of mental and emotional wellness. At the teacher's discretion, in certain discussions and activities, students may also be given the option of using the story as a jumping-off point for considering their own well-being, though this is never mandatory.

Additionally, the teacher guide offers a range of literacy-focused activities that enhance critical reading, writing, and communication skills, going beyond the text to encourage analytical thinking and creativity. It also encourages inquiry-based learning by posing thought-provoking questions and prompts that promote critical thinking and the exploration of issues related to Indigenous rights, cultural diversity, and societal inequalities. Furthermore, the guide fosters cultural awareness and respect by providing insights into the diverse cultures and traditions within Indigenous communities. Within the context of the novel, students will have the opportunity to self-reflect and explore their own values, biases, and beliefs.

As the writer of this guide, curriculum developer Christine M'Lot approached the sensitive nature of the topics explored in the novel by partnering with psychologist Dr. Karlee D. Fellner, who studies holistic Indigenous approaches to health. Together, they have created wellness lessons during which students will learn to see the events of the novel through the lens of survivance, exploring how the characters demonstrate strength and resilience even while dealing with trauma.

These wellness lessons introduce and build upon videos created by Dr. Fellner specifically for this teacher guide. In these videos, Dr. Fellner offers a series of teachings about wellness that guide students to understand and apply some of the holistic Indigenous approaches to health that she has developed in her practice and research. Further, in the "Teaching Difficult Topics From a Trauma-Informed Stance" section of this introduction, teachers will find a set of best practices that they are encouraged to use in their learning spaces and while teaching the topics in this teacher guide.

HOW THIS GUIDE IS STRUCTURED

The guide has five units: **Childhood, Adolescence**, **Adulthood Part 1**, **Adulthood Part 2**, and **Legacy**. These units correspond to portions of the novel's text, and mirror Indigenous theories of the stages of life. While Indigenous Nations have various ways of understanding and describing the stages of life, the general concept is that as humans, we move through the following stages:

- **Infancy and Childhood:** This stage marks the beginning of life and includes celebrations marking significant milestones including naming ceremonies. Babies are seen as gifts from the Creator, and their arrival is a cause for celebration. Families and communities play a crucial role in nurturing and educating children about their culture and traditions.
- **Adolescence:** As children grow, they transition into adolescence. This transition is often marked by initiation ceremonies (rites of passage) that help young people develop a sense of responsibility, identity, and their role within the community. Education about cultural heritage, responsibilities, and values is emphasized during this stage.

ISBN: 978-1-77492-094-7

- **Adulthood:** Adulthood in Indigenous cultures often involves additional rites of passage, such as marriage ceremonies. It is a time when individuals take on greater responsibilities within the community and may become parents themselves. The concept of giving back to the community and contributing to its well-being is a central theme.
- **Eldership:** Elders hold a special place in Indigenous communities. They are revered for their wisdom, experience, and knowledge. Elders often play a crucial role in decision-making, passing down traditions, and providing guidance to younger generations. This stage is seen as a time of reflection and sharing the wisdom gained over a lifetime.

Each unit is marked by a set of chapter readings and includes three lessons:

- Lesson 1: *Before* is a wellness activity that students will engage in prior to reading the section of text associated with the unit.
- Lesson 2: *During* focuses on comprehension and discussion, through which the topics in this section are debriefed and examined.
- Lesson 3: *After* is an inquiry activity where students will learn one step in the inquiry process. At the end of Unit 5: Legacy, students will complete and present a final inquiry project related to a topic in the novel.

ASSESSMENT

Effective assessment is a crucial component of the teaching and learning process. To support teachers, incorporated into this guide are various assessments designed to serve both formative and summative purposes. Assessments include student self-evaluations, exit slips, research worksheets, and the culminating inquiry project final assessment. These assessments are integrated into teaching to enhance student learning and gauge students' progress.

AUTHOR INTRODUCTIONS

INTRODUCTION TO THE AUTHOR: BEATRICE MOSIONIER

Beatrice Mosionier was born in St. Boniface, Manitoba, in 1949, and at the age of three became a ward of the Children's Aid Society. She grew up in a series of foster homes, separated from her birth family and her Métis heritage. After a short time living in Toronto, where she attended college, she returned to Winnipeg. Following the loss of two sisters to suicide, Beatrice decided to write *In Search of April Raintree* in the hopes of uncovering and expressing her personal insights. The story embodies her struggles in finding her cultural identity and relating to the world. First published in 1983, it has since become a Canadian classic. This heart-rending and powerful account illustrates the difficulties that many Indigenous Peoples face in maintaining a positive self-identity.

INTRODUCTION TO THE TEACHER GUIDE AUTHOR: CHRISTINE M'LOT

Christine M'Lot is an Anishinaabe educator, curriculum developer, and consultant from Winnipeg, Manitoba. She has written teacher guides for *This Place: 150 Years Retold*, *Sugar Falls*, and the Surviving the City series. She also co-edited an Indigenous education textbook called *Resurgence: Engaging With Indigenous Narratives and Cultural Expressions In and Beyond the Classroom* (2022).

INTRODUCTION TO THE TEACHER GUIDE WELLNESS CONSULTANT: DR. KARLEE D. FELLNER

Dr. Karlee D. Fellner is a citizen of the Métis Nation of Alberta. Dr. Fellner's areas of research and clinical expertise include Indigenous approaches to therapy and trauma work; holistic and traditional approaches to wellness; Indigenous research, curriculum, and pedagogy; culturally appropriate counselling; genocide-informed practice; and complex and intergenerational trauma. She is currently an associate professor of Counselling Psychology and Indigenous Education at the University of Calgary. Dr. Fellner is the founder and CEO of maskihkiy wellness, at <**www.maskihkiy.com**>, and a practising psychologist registered in Alberta. She is deeply involved in Indigenous leadership in mental health policy and practice.

INVITING AN ELDER INTO YOUR LEARNING SPACE

Teachers may want to engage the larger community and invite an Elder or Knowledge Keeper into their classroom to share stories, knowledge, or teachings. This can be a great way to highlight local Indigenous wellness philosophies, teachings, or practices. If you ask an Elder or Knowledge Keeper to share their own stories about attending residential school and their journey to healing, be aware that you are asking a person to speak about their trauma, and this is a conversation that should be approached with great care and sensitivity.

Manitoba Education and Youth defines an Elder as "any person regarded or chosen by an Aboriginal Nation to be the keeper and teacher of its oral tradition and knowledge," but it is important to remember that this definition may vary from community to community.[1] Some Indigenous keepers of knowledge are more comfortable being referred to as Traditional Knowledge Keepers than as Elders; be respectful of their preference. The following are some guidelines for building a positive relationship with a local Elder or Knowledge Keeper.

BEFORE THE MEETING

- Ask your school board or Indigenous Education lead if they have an Elder-in-residence or a trusted Elder or Knowledge Keeper whom they regularly ask to speak with students.

[1] Manitoba Education and Youth, *Integrating Aboriginal Perspectives Into Curricula.*

- Research the protocols in your community for inviting an Elder to speak with your class. If you are unsure about the protocols, ask the Elder what would be appropriate.
- Arrange a meeting to speak with the Elder well in advance of their planned visit to your class.

PLANNING THE VISIT

- In speaking with the Elder to plan their visit to your classroom, share a bit about yourself and your family's history.
- Listen to and learn from the Elder with intention.
- Adhere to the protocols in your area and ask the Elder if they would be interested in sharing their gifts with your class.
- Be as flexible about the day and time for the visit as you can. Decide this together!
- Ask if the Elder will need any special accommodations during their visit.
- Discuss fair compensation. The Elder may be taking time off work to accommodate your needs, so it is very important that they are well compensated for their time, energy, and emotional labour.
- Sometimes Elders appreciate it when they are given a list of questions from the students beforehand so they can plan their answers and only answer the questions they are comfortable addressing. This may be especially true if they are being asked about their experiences at residential school. Ask the Elder if this is their preference and follow through if so.

THE DAY OF THE VISIT

- Welcome the Elder to your class/school. Have a student volunteer present the Elder with an appropriate gift, such as a tobacco tie, depending on the protocol in your region.
- Give the Elder a tour of your school, if possible. At the very least, make sure they know where the washrooms are located.
- Ask the Elder how they would like to be introduced to your class.
- Ensure students are respectful while the Elder is speaking.
- Thank the Elder at the end of their visit and present them with their honorarium.

It is important to understand the significant contribution that Elders, Knowledge Keepers, and Indigenous communities make when they share their traditional knowledge. In their culture of reciprocity, this understanding should extend past giving a gift or honorarium to an Elder or Knowledge Keeper for sharing sacred knowledge. Think deeply about reciprocity and how you can go beyond inviting Indigenous guests to your classroom. Expand your own learning and become connected to Indigenous people by, for example, engaging in Indigenous community events, working with the education department of the local Nations, or exploring ways to continue developing the relationship between the local Nations and teachers in your board.

It is recommended that teachers build a relationship with a local Elder or Knowledge Keeper. Most schools have an Elder-in-residence who teachers can connect with. Relationships take time to develop, so teachers should contact the Elder as soon as possible. If the initial visit goes well, teachers should be sure to let the Elder know that they will be inviting the Elder back.

WHAT IS TRAUMA-INFORMED PRACTICE FOR TEACHERS?

Trauma-informed practice for teachers is working to understand how trauma can impact learning and behaviour, and applying that understanding to create safe classroom spaces for students. Although originally designed as a framework for delivering social services,[2] trauma-informed practice can be relevant to educational settings when students are learning about topics that could traumatize (or retraumatize) them. The goal of trauma-informed practice is to decrease the likelihood of traumatizing students while exposing them to traumatic narratives—such as those presented in the novel *April Raintree/In Search of April Raintree*. Examples of traumatic topics discussed in the novel include child welfare apprehensions, bullying, racism, addictions, sexual assault, and suicide. Great care has been taken to frame this story from an Indigenous and strength-based lens of *survivance*, a term discussed in the wellness lessons and coined by Indigenous scholar Gerald Vizenor who defines it as "an active sense of presence, the continuance of native stories, not a mere reaction, or a survivable name. Native survivance stories are renunciations of dominance, tragedy, and victimry."[3]

TEACHING DIFFICULT TOPICS FROM A TRAUMA-INFORMED STANCE

As is often true when learning about Indigenous subjects, sensitive topics may come up when students are reading, researching, or learning about the material in *April Raintree* and *In Search of April Raintree*. The story describes traumatic experiences such as being apprehended by child welfare services, bullying, addictions, sexual assault, and suicide.

Due to the prevalence of trauma in our world, it is very likely that someone in the class has experienced one or more of the types of trauma being discussed. We encourage educators

[2] See Butler, Critelli, and Rinfrette, "Trauma-Informed Care and Mental Health."

[3] Vizenor, Manifest Manners, vii.

to share a content warning with the class prior to engaging with the novel and give students the option to opt out of reading this novel if they think it will be too emotionally difficult. If a student chooses to opt out, note that it is at the educator's discretion to assign another novel for the student to study. A trauma-informed practice uses the utmost caution and care while teaching stories that include trauma. In this guide, each lesson includes an activity that supports student well-being while they read about these difficult topics.

Teaching about survivance from a trauma-informed stance means placing emphasis on informing students about resources available to them if they feel overwhelmed or triggered at any point. Throughout the process of preparing to read, reading, and responding to this story, teachers should create a safe and open learning environment where students' mental health is supported and boundaries are respected when learning about sensitive topics. Within lessons, there may be direct discussions about the concepts of mental health and wellness; if students are comfortable, these may be great opportunities to discuss and learn about positive coping skills that could be helpful when participating in this novel study. Students should always have the option of opting out of these discussions. Helpful information and advice on how to build flourishing learning communities and address mental health needs with all students can be found in *Ensouling Our Schools: A Universally Designed Framework for Mental Health, Well-Being, and Reconciliation* by Jennifer Katz with Kevin Lamoureux.

Below are some best practices to help educators teach with an awareness of and dedication to student wellness.

1. **Informed Consent and Communication:** A sample Parent/Guardian and Student Letter of Consent is available on page 13. Teachers are strongly encouraged to send this letter home with students prior to beginning the novel study. This letter, which informs parents/guardians and students about the content and objectives of the study, is centred around understanding trauma and promoting wellness in alignment with Indigenous principles of well-being. Open communication with parents and guardians is essential to building a supportive and understanding community around student learning experiences.

2. **Artistic Expression and Privacy:** During this novel study, students will have the opportunity to engage in wellness-focused artistic expression. It is crucial to emphasize that any wellness artwork created by students will not be graded or judged and should not be shared with the teacher or class unless a student voluntarily chooses to do so. Respecting their privacy and autonomy in this creative process is of utmost importance.

3. **Student Emotional Well-Being:** Students have the absolute right to disengage from any readings or lessons if they find them emotionally taxing. We encourage teachers to create a safe and open space where students feel comfortable expressing their emotions and concerns. It's essential to remind students that their emotional well-being is a priority, and they should not feel pressured to continue engaging with any content that causes them

distress. We leave it up to the teacher to engage students in alternative activities (either those provided within the lessons or of their own choice) that are appropriate for their classroom community and teaching goals.

4. **Collaborative Support:** Teachers are encouraged to collaborate with the school's guidance counsellor for the duration of these wellness-focused lessons. This partnership ensures that students have access to the guidance counsellor's support when needed and if they choose. A collaborative approach reinforces the message that seeking help and guidance is a sign of strength, not weakness.

By following these guidelines and promoting an environment of trust and understanding, educators can take steps toward creating a learning space where students may explore sensitive topics, such as trauma, in a way that aligns with Indigenous principles of wellness and promotes emotional healing and resilience.

[Your School Letterhead]
[Date]

Dear Parents/Guardians and Students,

Re: Upcoming Novel Study

We hope this letter finds you well. We are writing to inform you about an upcoming unit of study in [Teacher's Name]'s class that focuses on wellness and understanding trauma, with a particular emphasis on Indigenous principles of well-being. The unit is centred around the novel [*April Raintree or In Search of April Raintree*] and explores themes of trauma, resilience, and healing as portrayed in the book. This educational journey aligns with Indigenous principles of wellness and aims to provide students with a deeper understanding of these important concepts while reading a novel that includes traumatic experiences including child welfare apprehensions, bullying, racism, addictions, sexual assault, and suicide.

We have prepared this letter to seek your informed consent and to keep you informed about the content and objectives of this unit. We encourage you to engage in discussions with your child about their learning experiences and any questions or concerns they may have. During this unit, students will have the opportunity to engage in wellness-focused artistic expression. We want to emphasize that any wellness artwork created by students will not be graded or judged and will not be submitted to the teacher or for display unless the student voluntarily chooses to share it. This artwork may reflect their inner thoughts, feelings, and experiences as they navigate their understanding of trauma, or may reflect those of the characters in the novel, depending on each student's choice. We respect students' privacy and autonomy in this creative process.

Your child's emotional well-being is our utmost priority. If at any point during this unit your child feels that the content or discussions are emotionally taxing, they have the right to disengage. We encourage them to communicate their feelings with their teacher and seek support as needed. To provide the best support for our students, teachers will collaborate closely with our school's guidance counsellor throughout this unit. The guidance counsellor will be available to offer assistance and guidance to students as required and according to student preferences.

We believe that by fostering an environment of trust, understanding, and open communication, we can create a safe space for students to explore sensitive topics, such as trauma, in a way that aligns with Indigenous principles of wellness. Your support and partnership are greatly appreciated.

If you have any questions or concerns about this unit, please do not hesitate to reach out to [Teacher's Name] or our school's administration. We look forward to embarking on this educational journey with your child.

Sincerely,

[Principal's Name]
[School Name]
[Contact Information]

INQUIRY LEARNING

The lessons in this guide lead students through an inquiry project that culminates in a presentation of research they have done on a topic of interest. Scaffolded throughout the teacher guide are lessons that support student success by developing the research and critical-thinking skills necessary for engaging in inquiry through research.

- **Unit 1:** Students learn about the qualities of a good research question and then create their own research questions.
- **Unit 2:** Students learn about source reliability as they begin to investigate and refine their research questions.
- **Unit 3:** Students learn how to be critical while finding sources and apply this learning to their own research.
- **Unit 4:** Students learn the skills needed to effectively navigate and gather information from sources.
- **Unit 5:** Students learn what makes a great presentation and apply this learning to their own research presentations.

DEFINITIONS AND RESOURCES FOR STUDENTS AND EDUCATORS

Addiction: A treatable condition involving complex interactions among brain circuits, genetics, the environment, and an individual's life experiences.[4] Addiction offers a temporary relief from pain (physical, emotional, mental, and/or spiritual), and gives an individual a short-term sense of control and calmness. In the long term, addiction has many negative consequences; however, it is very difficult for the person experiencing the addiction to give it up, despite the consequences.[5]

To learn more:

Dr. Gabor Maté: Dr. Maté is a leading addictions expert who has done work demonstrating the roles of trauma, colonialism, and social inequality and injustice in addictions. A number of links to articles and videos are available on his website. https://drgabormate.com/addiction

[4] "Definition of Addiction," American Society of Addiction Medicine.

[5] "The Power of Addiction and the Addiction to Power | Gabor Maté, MD," *Mad in America: Science, Psychiatry and Social Justice.*

The Centre for Addiction and Mental Health (CAMH): CAMH is a leading Canadian research organization for mental health and addiction. They provide information and resources on addiction and its effects, including support for those who are struggling with addiction. **https://www.camh.ca**

Drug Free Kids Canada (DFKC): DFKC is a non-profit organization that provides information and resources on substance use and addiction, including educational materials and prevention strategies. **https://www.drugfreekidscanada.org**

Canadian Centre on Substance Use and Addiction (CCSA): CCSA was created through an act of Parliament in 1988 to develop a strategic plan toward fostering understanding and creating awareness of substance-use issues by creating accessible, evidence-informed publications. **https://ccsa.ca**

Alcoholics Anonymous (AA) and Narcotics Anonymous (NA): AA and NA are support groups that provide a community of individuals who are recovering from addiction and offer support, guidance, and accountability. <**https://www.aa.org**> and <**https://na.org**>.

Colonialism: The policy or practice of acquiring full or partial political control over another country, occupying it with settlers, and exploiting it economically.[6]

According to the *Highlights From the Report of the Royal Commission on Aboriginal Peoples*, colonization in Canada happened in four stages:[7]

Stage 1—Separate Worlds (up to 1500 AD): Indigenous and non-Indigenous societies developed on their own in lands far from each other, with different cultures and forms of social organization. This changed when Europeans arrived and began to settle in North America.

Stage 2—Contact and Co-operation (1500 to 1870): A growing non-Indigenous population sought ways to foster co-existence, mostly in the form of trading and military alliances. Despite a steep decline in Indigenous populations due to diseases carried by settlers, this time was marked by mutual tolerance and respect, with each society left to govern its own internal affairs.

[6] "Chapter 1: Terminology," *Indigenous Voices Online Learning Modules: Power and Privilege.*

[7] Royal Commission on Aboriginal Peoples, *Highlights From the Report.*

Stage 3—Displacement and Assimilation (1871 to 1969): In this period, most of non-Indigenous society—now larger and more dominant—stopped respecting their Indigenous neighbours. Interventions in the lives and lands of Indigenous Peoples grew as the dominant culture set up policies that forcefully absorbed Indigenous land and people into the Canadian mainstream.

Stage 4—Negotiation and Renewal (1970 to present): Supreme Court victories for Indigenous Peoples, along with the recognition that assimilation was a failure, compelled non-Indigenous society to begin seeking change to the relationship through dialogue, consultation, and negotiation. Meanwhile, Indigenous leaders regained greater control over their own affairs and re-established their own societies by healing the wounds caused by decades of domination.

Genocide: Article 2 of the United Nations Genocide Convention defines genocide as:

1. *A mental element*: the "intent to destroy, in whole or in part, a national, ethnical, racial or religious group, as such"; and
2. *A physical element*, which includes the following five acts, enumerated exhaustively:
   - Killing members of the group
   - Causing serious bodily or mental harm to members of the group
   - Deliberately inflicting on the group conditions of life calculated to bring about its physical destruction in whole or in part
   - Imposing measures intended to prevent births within the group
   - Forcibly transferring children of the group to another group[8]

Grief: The anguish experienced after significant loss, usually the death of a beloved person.[9] We experience intergenerational and vicarious grief through the losses that our families and communities have experienced. We may also grieve many other kinds of losses, such as loss of land, culture, language, animal relatives (e.g., pets), jobs, abilities (physical, intellectual, etc.), or anything else that is important to us.

[8] "Genocide," The United Nations Office on Genocide Prevention and the Responsibility to Protect.

[9] "Grief," *Psychology Topics*.

ISBN: 978-1-77492-094-7

To learn more:

Canadian Virtual Hospice: Canadian Virtual Hospice provides information and support for individuals and families facing end-of-life issues, including grief and bereavement. It offers a wide range of resources, including articles, videos, and online support groups. **https://www.virtualhospice.ca**

Kids Help Phone: This national helpline offers free, confidential support for young people across Canada. It provides resources and guidance on a range of issues, including grief and loss. **https://kidshelpphone.ca/get-info/im-grieving-a-loss-how-can-i-process-get-support**

Dougy Center: This organization offers resources and support for children, teens, and families who are grieving. It provides a variety of materials, including books, videos, and activity ideas, to help individuals cope with grief and loss. **https://www.dougy.org**

The Grief Toolbox: This online resource provides information and support for people who are grieving. It offers a variety of articles, podcasts, and videos on topics related to grief and bereavement. **https://thegrieftoolbox.com**

Homeostasis: A state of balance within the body. Homeostasis is maintained by all physical systems constantly adjusting in response to changes within or outside the body. The processes of cleansing and clearing are important for maintaining homeostasis.

Indigenous Peoples: "Indigenous Peoples" is a collective name for the original peoples of North America and their descendants. The Canadian Constitution recognizes three groups of Indigenous Peoples: First Nations, Métis, and Inuit.[10]

To learn more:

The Peoples Atlas of Canada: *The Indigenous Peoples Atlas of Canada* is an English and French educational resource created by the Royal Canadian Geographical Society, published by Canadian Geographic and funded by the Government of Canada. The Atlas consists of a four-volume set, an interactive website, five floor maps, downloadable tile maps, plastic-coated maps, poster maps, teaching guides for elementary and secondary school students, and lesson plans. **https://indigenouspeoplesatlasofcanada.ca/article/identity/**

[10] "Indigenous Peoples and Communities," Crown-Indigenous Relations and Northern Affairs Canada.

  ISBN: 978-1-77492-094-7

Internalized racism: Absorbing or accepting the negative stereotypes, values, images, and ideologies perpetuated by the white dominant society about one's racial group.[11]

Métis: A mixed-race group that has ancestry that is Indigenous (usually Cree, Saulteaux, and Dene) and European/Euro-Canadian (usually French Canadian, Scots, and Orcadian).[12] A community of people who self-identify as being Métis and are of historic Métis Nation ancestry.[13] This community is one of the three groups of Indigenous Peoples recognized in Canada, along with Inuit and First Nations peoples.

To learn more:

Métis Minute: Métis Minute is an informative video series focusing not only on Red River Métis culture and history but also on the departments, affiliates, and programs of the Manitoba Métis Federation (MMF). These short videos highlight the MMF's extensive, diverse programs and services, celebrate the strength of the Métis people, and encapsulate what makes the Red River Métis who they are today. **https://www.mmf.mb.ca/metis-minute**

Survivance: A term coined by Anishinaabe scholar Gerald Vizenor, who defines it as "an active sense of presence, the continuance of native stories, not a mere reaction, or a survivable name. Native survivance stories are renunciations of dominance, tragedy, and victimry."[14]

To learn more:

"iskotew & crow: (re)igniting narratives of Indigenous survivance & trauma w/ Dr. Karlee Fellner": In this video posted by the **Simon Fraser University** Department of Psychology, Dr. Fellner tells the story of Iskotew and the Crow, and goes into depth on the teachings of the story. **https://www.youtube.com/watch?v=47oj13edpSo**

Additional learning is also available through Dr. Fellner's book chapter, "Iskotew & Crow: Reigniting Narratives of Indigenous Survivance and Trauma Wisdom in the Classroom" (see "Resources for Teachers and Students" on page 94).

Trauma: A physical, mental, social, and/or spiritual response to experiencing or witnessing a life-threatening or physically or emotionally harmful event or series of events or circumstances. Harmful events or circumstances may "include natural disasters, serious accidents, terrorist

---

[11] Pyke, "What Is Internalized Racial Oppression and Why Don't We Study It?"

[12] "Métis Identity," *Indigenous Peoples Atlas of Canada.*

[13] "Citizenship Application—FAQ's," Manitoba Métis Federation.

[14] Vizenor, *Manifest Manners*, vii.

acts, war/combat, rape/sexual assault, historical trauma, intimate partner violence, and bullying."[15] The complex, collective trauma that Indigenous Peoples have experienced due to the many acts of attempted genocide since contact with settlers is also referred to as ancestral trauma, historical trauma, colonial trauma, and the soul wound. These terms acknowledge the compound intergenerational traumas that Indigenous people experience even when they do not witness or directly experience a traumatic event themselves.[16]

To learn more:

The Canadian Mental Health Association (CMHA): The CMHA provides information and resources on mental health and trauma, including educational materials, support groups, and counselling services. **https://cmha.ca**

The Centre for Addiction and Mental Health (CAMH): CAMH is a leading Canadian research organization for mental health and addiction. It provides information and resources on trauma and its effects, including support for those who have experienced trauma. **https://www.camh.ca**

Kids Help Phone: This national helpline offers free, confidential support for young people across Canada. It provides resources and guidance on a range of issues, including grief and loss. **https://kidshelpphone.ca/get-info/im-grieving-a-loss-how-can-i-process-get-support**

Hope for Wellness Helpline: This free, confidential support service provides counselling and resources for Indigenous people in Canada who are experiencing trauma or other mental health issues. **https://www.hopeforwellness.ca**

The Mood Disorders Society of Canada (MDSC): MDSC provides resources and support for individuals dealing with mental health issues, including trauma. **https://mdsc.ca**

---

[15] "What is Posttraumatic Stress Disorder (PTSD)?" American Psychiatric Association.

[16] Fellner et al., "Counselling Indigenous peoples in a Canadian context," 123–147.

1

CHILDHOOD (CHAPTERS 1–4)

UNIT OVERVIEW

Before reading these chapters, students will participate in a wellness activity designed to help them "connect and protect" when hearing stories that include traumatic events. Then, as students read chapters 1–4, they will answer comprehension questions and engage in small-group discussions about themes and topics in the novel. Finally, students will create effective research questions to guide their inquiry.

Note: The letter of consent (page 13) should be sent to parents and guardians before teaching this unit.

INFORMATION FOR TEACHERS: THE HISTORY AND LEGACY OF RESIDENTIAL SCHOOLS

It is impossible to overstate the significance of the history and legacy of residential schools in Canada. Between 1867 and 1996, at least 150 000 children were taken from their homes and sent to government-funded, church-run schools.[17] Below are some key points in history that teachers are encouraged to explore further.

[17] "The Residential School System," Parks Canada.

  ISBN: 978-1-77492-094-7

- John A. Macdonald, Canada's founding prime minister, is regarded as the architect of the residential school system and for this reason is a controversial figure in Canadian history.[18] While many Canadians—past and present—believe that the sole purpose of these schools was to educate Indigenous children and help them integrate into settler society, in actuality it was to eliminate Indigenous culture as an act of cultural genocide. The result was catastrophic and continues to negatively affect Indigenous people to this day. Through the residential school system, the government alienated children from their families, culture, language, spirituality, and land, ultimately causing the breakdown of the family unit.
- The history of interactions between Indigenous Peoples and what would become Canada is complicated. Indigenous Nations helped French and British settlers navigate the unfamiliar terrain and showed them how to survive during the harsh winter months.[19] Many Indigenous Nations had lucrative trade deals with the French and British.[20] Some Indigenous Nations, such as the Shawnee, even fought alongside the British against the United States in the War of 1812, curbing US expansion into Canada.[21] Even more fascinatingly, a group of Mohawk men went on a military expedition with the British in 1884 to Egypt to rescue the former British Governor General of Canada from Sudanese forces.[22] Although British and Canadian allyship with Indigenous Nations cannot be overlooked, the British broke many of the promises that they made to the Indigenous Nations.
- The 1867 Indian Act defined life for Indigenous Peoples for over a hundred years, and arguably continues to do so. Through the Indian Act—a race-based legislation—Indigenous people could not vote, run for office, hire lawyers, or even use farming equipment. The Indian Act also paved the way for the residential school system.
- While education was important to Indigenous people and leaders advocated for education to be included in the various treaties, Indigenous families did not have a choice in sending their children to residential schools. They were often threatened with jail time if they hesitated to send their children.
- Today, we continue to see the ongoing traumatic effects of residential schools, which produced generations of Indigenous people who struggle with identity, cultural pride, and community.

---

[18] Carleton, "John A. Macdonald."

[19] Lackenbauer et al., "The Arrival of the Europeans."

[20] "First Nations in Canada," Crown-Indigenous Relations and Northern Affairs Canada.

[21] Miller, "Indigenous-British Relations Pre-Confederation."

[22] Benn, *Mohawks on the Nile*.

  ISBN: 978-1-77492-094-7

"LEANING INTO THE LAND" WELLNESS ACTIVITY

Goals of These Activities: Before reading chapters 1–4, students will engage in a series of activities designed to support their wellness while reading and learning about difficult topics. Through the wellness activity below, students will learn about leaning into the land and the concept of "connect and protect."

Note: Be sure to review the content of the novels and share the content warnings prior to beginning the novel study.

MATERIALS

- internet access
- projector
- My Wellness Toolbox reproducible (page 26, one for each student)
- paper
- art supplies (e.g., drawing paper, markers, paints, paintbrushes, pencil crayons)

DURATION

1.5–2 Hours

THE LESSON

ACTIVATE: THINK/PAIR/SHARE

Begin the lesson by informing students that they are going to read a novel that deals with trauma. To help them process this novel in a safe way, they are also going to learn about wellness from an Indigenous perspective. Inform the group of the ways you as the educator are going to care for their wellness during this novel study. For example, teachers may collaborate with the school's guidance counsellor for the duration of the wellness-focused lessons. Students can have access to the guidance counsellor's support when needed and if they choose. Explain that whenever you ask a student a question, they are free to answer in a general way and do not have to share any personal experiences or wellness strategies they are not comfortable sharing.

Begin the lesson by asking students to brainstorm some general ways people can connect with the land for wellness (e.g., spending time outdoors, hiking, swimming, being with animals). Encourage them to identify land-based activities they believe can positively impact one's well-being.

Next, have students think about these activities and reflect on how they might make someone feel good or contribute to their overall wellness. Instead of sharing personal experiences, have students discuss these general ideas and the potential benefits with the person next to them. This will promote a broader understanding of the topic and encourage students to consider the wellness aspects of connecting with the land without delving into personal stories.

Solicit volunteers to share their ideas with the group. Share your experiences as well.

Review key vocabulary that Dr. Fellner uses in the video "Leaning Into the Land" (16:00) at <https://youtu.be/6sqllp91y0o> such as *homeostasis*, *Indigenous Peoples*, and *colonialism*. (Students will view this video in the following section, Acquire.)

ACQUIRE: VIDEO INTRODUCTION TO "LEANING INTO THE LAND"

Introduce students to Dr. Fellner's video "Leaning Into the Land." Say:

- According to Indigenous theories of wellness, our bodies have natural ways of maintaining wellness through difficult times, including by going to the land. We are now going to watch a video by Dr. Fellner, a Métis psychologist who specializes in Indigenous psychotherapy. In the video, Dr. Fellner shares ways we can go to the land for wellness and healing in times of trouble. In particular, we are going to learn how we can "connect and protect" when hearing difficult stories—such as those involving trauma—and learn how to recognize when characters in the novel do the same.

Share Dr. Fellner's video "Leaning Into the Land" (16:00), encouraging students to listen for the tips she shares on how to connect with the land for healing and how animals and plants use the land to achieve homeostasis.

After the video, have students reflect on what they learned. Ask:

- What was the example Dr. Fellner gave of animals using the land to achieve homeostasis?
- How does this connect to the think/pair/share brainstorming and reflection?
- Can anyone give examples of Indigenous ceremonies practised where we live?
- How might these ceremonies contribute to wellness?

Then, ask:

- What were the tips Dr. Fellner gave us on how we can go to the land for healing?

Record answers on the board so students can refer back to them later in the lesson.

APPLY: LEANING INTO THE LAND IN MY OWN LIFE: GUIDED EXPERIENCE

Next, share Dr. Fellner's video "Land-Based Check-In" (12:30) at <https://youtu.be/3-bsNbpzlA0>, which leads viewers into a mindfulness-meditation-like experience.

After the video, ask students to individually reflect on how they felt while engaging in the meditation.

Review the concept of medicine as shared by Dr. Fellner. Say:

- In the first video, Dr. Fellner defines medicine as "anything that helps us come into balance in a good way." Spend some time thinking about what activities in your life act as medicine for you.

Provide each student with one copy of the My Wellness Toolbox reproducible (page 26) and have students use the space provided to draw or write down different "medicines" (i.e., activities and actions that a person can use to bring them into balance in a good way). Examples may include "connecting and protecting," playing sports, participating in guided meditation, spending time with family and/or friends, creating art, playing with a pet, reading, practising their personal spirituality and/or religion, cooking, or experiencing land-based activities, such as going for a walk.

Students should reflect on the following questions:

- What brings you into balance in a good way?
- What piece of land and/or medicines came up for you during the meditation?

Encourage students to refer to the list of tips Dr. Fellner provided on how to go to the land for healing.

Allow students 25 minutes to complete their toolbox, which will serve as a menu of options for them to turn to while engaging in the novel study. Remind students that they do not have to share their toolboxes with anyone, including the teacher.

ASSESS/REFLECT: REFLECTION

Finally, have students reflect on the activity, either in private writing that does not need to be submitted or in paired discussions. Sample reflection prompts include:

- Share something from your toolbox that a person can use while engaging in this novel study.
- What did you think about your participation in the guided meditation?
- How has your idea of the concept of wellness changed throughout this lesson?

Name: ______________________________ Date: ______________________________

MY WELLNESS TOOLBOX

Use the space provided to draw or write down some different "medicines" (i.e., activities and actions that you can use to bring yourself into balance in a good way). Examples may include "connecting and protecting," playing sports, participating in guided meditation, spending time with family and/or friends, creating art, playing with a pet, reading, practising your personal spirituality and/or religion, cooking, or experiencing land-based activities, such as going for a walk.

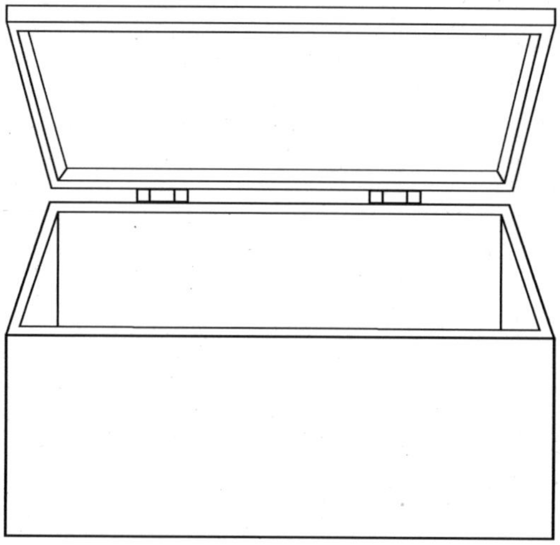

 ISBN: 978-1-77492-094-7

1.1.1

INTRODUCTION TO REFLECTION, DISCUSSION, AND INQUIRY

Goals of These Activities: Students will actively read chapters 1–4 by taking notes, marking important passages, and asking questions as they read. Students will be able to summarize the plot and themes of *April Raintree/In Search of April Raintree*, analyze the characters and their experiences, and discuss the social and historical context of the novel.

INFORMATION FOR TEACHERS: ABOUT THE AUTHOR

Beatrice Mosionier was born in St. Boniface, Manitoba, in 1949, and at the age of three became a ward of the Children's Aid Society. She grew up in foster homes, away from her birth family and her Métis heritage. After a short time living in Toronto, where she attended college, she returned to Winnipeg. Following the loss of two sisters to suicide, Beatrice decided to write *In Search of April Raintree* in the hopes of finding personal insights. The story embodies her personal struggles for identity and relating to the world. First published in 1983, it has become a Canadian classic. The heart-rending and powerful account presents the difficulties that many Indigenous people face in maintaining a positive self-identity. In 1984, Mosionier published *April Raintree*, a version of the novel that was adapted for high-school students.

MATERIALS

- internet access
- projector
- copies of the novel *April Raintree* or *In Search of April Raintree*
- close-reading materials (e.g., highlighters, sticky notes)
- Discussion Participation Scale reproducible (page 30; one copy for each student)

DURATION

1–2 Hours

THE LESSON

ACTIVATE: ABOUT THE AUTHOR

Before beginning the novel, show the video in which the author, Beatrice Mosionier, introduces herself and reads from *In Search of April Raintree.*

Read "Information for Teachers: About the Author" (page 27) and show the video "The Author's Note from 'In Search of April Raintree' read by Beatrice Mosionier" (7:13) at <https://www.youtube.com/watch?v=h1RSqyadJ0E>.

Next, ask students:

- What terms, experiences, and emotions do you predict may be relevant to the story?

Discuss student responses.

Then, solicit volunteers to share a wellness activity from their toolbox from the previous wellness lesson that they or their classmates can use if they feel it may be helpful to them at any point while reading the novel.

ACQUIRE: READ CHAPTERS 1–4

Assign students the task of individually reading chapters 1–4. Encourage students to take notes, mark important passages, and ask questions as they read.

Encourage students to mark sections that relate to the author's biography, and to notice when April first experiences racism.

APPLY: SMALL-GROUP DISCUSSIONS

Once students have read the chapters, provide each student with a copy of the Discussion Participation Scale reproducible (page 30). Review the discussion behaviours that students should strive for under "Active Involvement."

Organize the class into small groups to discuss the events of the novel and analyze the characters and themes. Encourage students to share their thoughts and ideas and facilitate a respectful and inclusive discussion. Provide students with questions and prompts, and allow groups approximately 2–3 minutes to discuss each question before having one person from the group summarize their conversation for the whole class.

Sample discussion prompts include:

1. Share one of your marked passages with your group. What stood out to you in this section and why?
2. Discuss the concept of narrator reliability. *Narrator reliability* refers to how reliable the narrator is in giving readers an accurate description of events. Because April is describing her

analysis of the situation and how she understood it as a child, what gaps in information are there? What misunderstandings are present in this section?

3. How does the author's description of white children show how she feels about herself and her own race? What examples of overt racism (openly apparent racism) are discussed in this section? How might this relate to the author's personal experiences?
4. How does the author's experience at the orphanage compare to a residential school experience you may have heard about before?
5. How does April's internalized racism (i.e., believing negative stereotypes about her race) affect her identity formation and goals for her future?
6. Are there examples of April "leaning into the land" in this section? What are they?
7. What questions do you have so far about the themes and topics in these chapters?

ASSESS: DISCUSSION PARTICIPATION SCALE

After the group discussions, have students complete the Discussion Participation Scale to track their own engagement in the small-group discussions. Collect the completed Discussion Participation Scales for formative assessment and return. When evaluating completed Discussion Participation Scales, note that some students may have chosen to opt out of certain discussions due to the subject matter. Therefore, formative assessments should be evaluated based on thoughtfulness and honesty, rather than participation in discussions.

Remind students that they are practising their group discussion skills throughout this novel study and will complete a Discussion Participation Scale after each unit's discussion to track their progress and reflect on their developing skills. Have students retain their completed Discussion Participation Scales for use at the end of Unit 5.

ISBN: 978-1-77492-094-7

Name: ____________________ Date: ____________________

DISCUSSION PARTICIPATION SCALE

Once the group discussion concludes, take a few minutes to reflect on your participation in the small-group discussion.

Grade	Discussion Qualities
1 **Limited Involvement**	• Demonstrated limited knowledge of the reading • Tried to respond when called on but didn't offer much insight • Demonstrated infrequent involvement in the discussion
2 **Sporadic Involvement**	• Demonstrated some knowledge of the reading • Offered straightforward facts and information about the reading • Contributed a moderate degree when called upon in the group discussion • Demonstrated sporadic involvement in the discussion
3 **Consistent Involvement**	• Demonstrated thorough knowledge of the reading • Offered interpretations and analysis of the events in the novel • Responded to other students' points of view and comments • Asked group members questions • Demonstrated consistent involvement in the discussion
4 **Active Involvement**	• Demonstrated superior knowledge of the reading • Offered insightful interpretations, analysis, and evaluation of events in the novel • Acted as a leader in the group discussion and responded to other students' points of views, asked group members questions, and called on less-involved group members to speak • Demonstrated very active involvement in the discussion

My Participation Grade: __/4

Explanation:

DEVELOPING A RESEARCH QUESTION

Goals of These Activities: After reading the first section of the novel, students will be introduced to their culminating inquiry project. The first skill they will learn is developing a research question in order to further their inquiry.

MATERIALS

- internet access
- Crafting, Refining, and Using an Effective Research Question reproducible (page 35; one copy for each student)
- Unit 1 Exit Slip reproducible (page 37; one copy for each student)

DURATION

1.5–2 Hours

 ISBN: 978-1-77492-094-7

THE LESSON

ACTIVATE: IMAGE ACTIVATION

To begin the lesson, introduce the topic of residential schools in Canada to the class. Say:

- Residential schools in Canada operated between 1867 and 1996. At least 150 000 children were taken from their homes and sent to government-funded, church-run schools.[23] Students at these schools often faced many types of abuses, including physical abuse, emotional abuse, and sexual abuse, and students were actively discouraged from practising their culture and speaking their traditional language.

Inform the class that learning about the residential school system in Canada will help them understand the historical context of the novel.

Next, show the class an image of a residential school. Find images of the closest school to you by viewing the residential school locator using CBC's Interactive Map at <https://www.cbc.ca/news2/interactives/beyond-94-residential-school-map/>.

Once you've identified the residential school closest to you, find an image of the school online. Display the image to the class.

Ask students to record all the questions that come to mind when they look at the image. Allow them 4–5 minutes to reflect and write before asking students to share their questions with the class. Create a list of questions on the board that includes all suggestions.

ACQUIRE: WHAT MAKES AN EFFECTIVE RESEARCH QUESTION?

Distribute a copy of the Crafting, Refining, and Using an Effective Research Question reproducible (page 35) to each student. Choose one of the class-generated questions from the previous activity. Together with the class, review this question according to the nine characteristics of an effective research question listed on the reproducible. Then, model how the question could be revised in order to make it more effective. The point is not to criticize the question but to identify its potential and demonstrate how revising it can make it stronger.

Choose two more questions that have some, but not all, of the characteristics of effective research questions. Organize the class into small groups and have students work within their groups to revise both questions to match all the criteria of effective research questions.

[23] Miller, "Residential Schools in Canada."

APPLY: CRAFT AN EFFECTIVE RESEARCH QUESTION

Inform students that they will now create research questions on topics presented or discussed so far in the novel study. Brainstorm topics that have come up in their reading and discussion, and list them on the board (e.g., addiction, internalized racism, colonization and its effects on the present day, taking care of ourselves while experiencing or learning about trauma). Explain that they will each select a topic that interests them and then, working in small groups with two to three other students who have selected the same or a similar topic, they will create a research question.

Throughout this study, students will have opportunities to gather information that will help them answer this question through research and inquiry and share the information with their group members. At the end of the study, they will make a short (maximum 10 minutes) group presentation to the class on what they have learned. They will also have opportunities to revise or refine their questions in response to new information.

Model this process by showing examples of research questions that could be developed from one or two of the topics on the board. Point out that many different research questions can be developed from a single topic. Note that students may ask questions about particular characters in the novel. Encourage them to keep asking these questions as they read, but also to think about themes and issues more generally for their research. For example, if a student asks the question, "Why do April and Cheryl's parents consume alcohol?" you could help them reframe the question as, "What are some reasons people consume alcohol to an extent that negatively impacts their lives?" Here are some other examples.

- Addiction: What are some of the ways addiction affects relationships? What are some effective ways of healing from addiction?
- Self-Care: Why are healthy relationships important, and how can we form them? What are the qualities of a healthy parent-child relationship, and how can these be developed and nurtured? What are good ways to take care of ourselves and each other in times of pain?
- Racism: What causes internalized racism? What are some effective ways of protecting ourselves from the effects of racism?
- Trauma: How does trauma affect people? How can people heal from trauma and become stronger?
- Survivance: What are some of the ways Indigenous people can maintain an "active sense of presence"? Why is "the continuance of native stories" important to survivance?

For further information regarding these and other topics, see "Definitions and Resources for Students and Educators" in the introduction (page 14).

Have students work in small groups to draft two research questions per brainstorming topic on the board. Walk around the room and assist as needed.

Once students have completed the task, have volunteers share some of the effective research questions they've come up with. Have the class discuss whether the question is effective or not. If not, spend time revising the question to fit the criteria. Record the research questions on chart paper or in an online document.

Post all the research questions where students can see them and where you can refer to them in future classes.

ASSESS: EXIT SLIP

Explain to students that they will complete an Exit Slip to demonstrate their understanding of developing research questions, and that the research questions they develop will be shared with the class. Hand out a Unit 1 Exit Slip reproducible (page 37) to each student. Have students record the research question they find the most compelling at this point. (Note: Students are not bound to this question for their inquiry project and will have opportunities to refine or revise their research questions in later units so that one question is focused on for the culminating inquiry project.)

Students will hand in the Exit Slip at the end of class.

Assign students to small inquiry project groups of two to three students based on their topics of interest. Inform them that they will need to agree on a single research question before they begin Unit 5, but they will have time to reflect and discuss before then.

Name: ______________________ Date: ______________________

CRAFTING, REFINING, AND USING AN EFFECTIVE RESEARCH QUESTION

The questions in this checklist will help refine the focus of your question and organize your research for your inquiry project. You may review questions according to the nine characteristics of an effective research question listed below. Then, use the characteristics to revise each question in order to make it more effective.

Remember: the point is not to criticize the question but to identify its potential and demonstrate how revising it can make it stronger and more useful in your culminating inquiry project.

1. Are you passionate about the topic of the question?
    - The question you come up with should pique your interest, fuelling your motivation to delve deeper. Your personal connection will transform your research from a chore into an exciting adventure.
    - Choosing a topic that genuinely interests you will ensure you care about finding the answer.
2. Does the question encourage you to think deeply about new ideas or topics?
    - The answers to the question you come up with should not be easily found and should require in-depth thought.
    - Finding the answers to the question should require some research.
3. Does the question avoid predetermined answers or limited perspectives?
    - In developing a question, embrace the unknown and allow your research to unfold, shaping your understanding of the topic along the way.

      For example, does the question cover a topic you are already very familiar with? If it does, is there a new perspective to be found in that topic? Or is there another topic that could challenge your own understanding better?
4. Does the question steer clear of simple "yes" or "no" answers?
    - Seek a question that prompts insightful explanations and encourages you to explore the "why" behind each subject, idea, or theme.
5. Can you approach the question with an open mind?
    - Approach your inquiry and research with an open mind and be ready to be surprised by what you discover. This will help you avoid falling into predetermined answers and limited perspectives in your thinking, and later, in your research.

  ISBN: 978-1-77492-094-7

6. Can the question be focused, even though it may initially have many possible answers?
   > Sharpen your focus. A broad question might be a great starting point, but to achieve focused exploration, it must be refined. Imagine your question as a laser beam, precisely targeting the aspect you want to illuminate.

   For example, the question "What were the effects of the residential school system on Indigenous Peoples?" can have many different answers based on the type of person affected, the period in their life, and their experience in the residential school system. By focusing the question on one of these routes of exploration, the answer can be more thoughtful and nuanced, better reflecting the research.

7. Can the question be reasonably answered?
   > Consider the feasibility of answering your question. Ensure your question has answers within reach. While you can explore new frontiers, make sure credible information exists to guide your journey.

8. Does the question include terms that can be defined?
   > Remember to define terms that appear in your question. Ensure the meaning of all terms is clear before you begin your inquiry and research.

   For example, if you're using phrases like "latest" or "most recent," make sure you specify a timeframe in the question. This will help to further focus your question, and thus, inquiry and research.

9. Does your initial question lead to further questions?
   > Remember, inquiry is a never-ending cycle. As you gather information, new questions will emerge, sparking further exploration and deeper understanding. It's okay to end with more questions than you started with.

This reproducible adapted from Dale Roy, Erika Kustra, and Paola Borin. "What Is a 'Good' Inquiry Question?" McMaster University, 2003. https://cll.mcmaster.ca/resources/misc/good_inquiry_question.html

Name: ______________________________ Date: ______________________________

UNIT 1 EXIT SLIP

The research question I find most compelling so far is:

2

ADOLESCENCE (CHAPTERS 5–7)

UNIT OVERVIEW

Before reading chapters 5–7, students will participate in a wellness activity designed to help them understand and reflect on the topic of survivance. Next, students will read chapters 5–7 of the novel, while answering comprehension questions and engaging in small-group discussions about the themes and topics in the novel and how they relate to the larger historical context. Finally, students will learn how to determine whether a source is reliable when conducting research and how to apply that learning as they investigate their research questions.

ISBN: 978-1-77492-094-7

"TRANSFORMATION AND SURVIVANCE" WELLNESS ACTIVITY

Goals of These Activities: Before reading chapters 5–7, students will engage in an activity designed to support their wellness while reading and learning about difficult topics. In this activity, students will learn about the topics of transformation and survivance in order to independently identify threads of survivance throughout the novel.

MATERIALS

- internet access
- projector
- Iskotew and Crow Story reproducible (page 42; one copy for each student)

DURATION

1.5 Hours

TEACHER GUIDE FOR APRIL RAINTREE AND IN SEARCH OF APRIL RAINTREE © 2024 CHRISTINE M'LOT © 2024 DR. KARLEE D. FELLNER (WELLNESS ACTIVITIES) ISBN: 978-1-77492-094-7

THE LESSON

ACTIVATE: WORD SPLASH—WHAT DOES IT MEAN TO *SURVIVE*?

Before beginning the lesson, inform the class that they will be learning about a concept called *survivance*. Begin by creating word splashes to determine prior knowledge students have about the words *survival* and *resilience*. Record *survival* on one side of the board and *resilience* on the other side. Ask:

- What comes to mind when you think of the word *survival*?

Record students' responses on the board. Then, ask:

- What comes to mind when you think of the word *resilience*?

Record students' responses on the board.

ACQUIRE: "TRANSFORMATION AND SURVIVANCE" VIDEO

Show Dr. Fellner's video "Transformation and Survivance" (9:06) at <https://youtu.be/Pk-3hgrAjbE>.

After watching the video, revisit the word splashes. Have students add to the word splash new words that they've learned about *survival* and *resilience*. What new words did they add to the board? How has their understanding of *survival*, *resilience*, *survivance*, and *transformation* evolved from this activity?

Dr. Fellner provides Gerald Vizenor's definition of his term *survivance* as "an active sense of presence. The continuance of native stories, not a mere reaction or survivable name. Native survivance stories are renunciations of dominance, tragedy, and victory."[24] Dr. Fellner summarizes the term as describing "the ways Indigenous Peoples have survived and thrived on the land for thousands of years."

APPLY: CROW STORY AND DISCUSSION

Hand out copies of the Iskotew* and Crow Story reproducible to each student. Inform students that this is a story that was given to Dr. Fellner through ceremony to teach people a different way of being with suffering and difficulty. Inform the group that this story is not meant to discourage modern ways of dealing with suffering and illness, such as taking medication; rather, the story illustrates an Indigenous psychotherapeutic perspective on suffering and difficulty. Give students time to silently read the story.

  ISBN: 978-1-77492-094-7

[24] Dr. Fellner is quoting Vizenor, *Manifest Manners*, vii.

* Pronounced "isk – oh – tay – oh." Note: iskotew means "fire" in Plains Cree (Y-dialect Cree).

Once students have individually read the story, organize them into small groups to discuss the following questions:

1. What are your initial thoughts about the story?
2. How did you feel about the way Iskotew learns to shift her understanding of the difficulties she's experiencing?
3. How does this view differ from the way society typically treats the difficulties people experience (e.g., anxiety, depression, trauma, other health issues)?
4. How does Iskotew demonstrate "survivance" in the story?
5. What lessons can we take from the story?

ASSESS/REFLECT: SURVIVANCE IN MY OWN LIFE

Have students write an independent journal reflection in response to the following prompt:

- Describe the skills, resources, and wisdom you've learned from some of the difficulties in your life or that you have learned from observing someone else handle difficulties in their life. This can include one of the characters from the novel if you choose.

Remind students that they do not have to show their journal reflection to anyone, including you.

  ISBN: 978-1-77492-094-7

ISKOTEW AND CROW STORY

SQUAAAAAWK SQUAAAAAWK SQUAAAAAWK

it was barely sunrise and that pesky crowalarm wouldn't let her sleep
"UGHHHHHHHH!!!" Iskotew let out a huuuuuuge groan
she flip-flopped in her bed pillow over her head but crow was too loud

"fine! I'm getting up!!" she declared to the empty space around her

that crow had been harassing her for so long now Iskotew couldn't remember how far back it began heck almost felt like it started before her lifetime

either way details didn't matter
what mattered was that damn crow had gone too far and was still going
it was ruining her life and she was sickofit
cawing pecking squawking talking relentless!

she'd tried everything in the books
politely asking the crow to leave yelling at it to go away throwing things at it
feeding it desperately pleading with it
she even went to dr.crowwhisperer supposedly professionally trained to get rid of crows
but at best dr.crowwhisperer could only distract the crow momentarily

the crow had become so disruptive that Iskotew had even tried her last resort
she went to see dr.coyote one day looking all dapper in his suit n white lab coat
see even tho dr.coyote had a reputation as an expert Iskotew was wary of dr.coyotes
but she'd tried everything in the books and noneofit worked
so into dr.coyote's office she went

"what's the problem?" dr.coyote grinned

"it's this crow won't leave me alone trying to figure out what to do about it"
dr.coyote's grin spread so wide it almost fell off his face
he rifled thru his pockets "aha!" he pulled out a tiny pill

This story was originally published in *Knowing the Past, Facing the Future: Indigenous Education in Canada*, edited by S. Carr-Stewart and J. Ottmann (UBC Press, 2019, pp. 143–170). Some revisions were made with permission from the author.

"just take this! It'll get rid of that crow in no time" dr.coyote winked tossed the pill to Iskotew
"hmmm..." Iskotew examined the pill fakesmiled "thanks dr.coyote"
dr.coyote's grin grew so big there was no beginning or end he nodded
warningsideeffectsmayinclude apathy silencing lowselfworth fear learnedhelplessness disconnection oppression suppression

indeed dr.coyote's pill helped shut that crow up
well more like Iskotew couldn't hear it anymore
the crow was still around all the time it was just muffled
problem was so was everything else
Iskotew couldn't see hear feel taste smell experience much of anything anymore!
and she was still so tired so heavy so sickofit
eventually crow just got louder anyway caw CAW CAW! Above the pills
so she gave up and threw em away

seemed everyone around Iskotew was sickofit too
that crow followed her to family dinners school work
she couldn't even hang out with her friends without that pesky crow showing up
everyone at school knew her as crowgirl one teacher warned the next
lest they GASP!! be surprised when crowgirl entered their class
seemed Iskotew's path as crowgirl was set
she kept her head down headphones in spent most of her time in the dark alone

some grew impatient "crowgirl! I'm sick of you and your crow! I don't wanna hear about it!"
others felt sorry for her "poor crowgirl you never did anything to deserve this sad enit"
some blamed her "what's wrong with you? how long's it been?! get rid of that crow already!!"
still others tried to rescue her by going after the crow
sssshhhhhhhushing it swinging at it yelling at it ignoring it feeding it
you name it they tried it all
and got exhausted

everyone seemed to have their own take on how to get rid of that problematic crow
and nothing worked crow just got louder louder louder LOUDER

crowgirl had been sickofit long enough her last resort had failed nothing seemed to help
so that morning as the sun rose crowgirl got up with determination
"I'M DONE WITH YOU CROW!!" she yelled angrily

crowgirl charged out the door no destination   she was just done
notacare   where she might end up   or whether she returned

her feet pounded out a dancedrumbeat on the sidewalk
her steps   lighter   heavier   lighter again
"LET'S GO!" she thoughtgiggled to herself
a crazyfeeling of   renewed energy   nonsensical optimism   movement

crowgirl walked and walked and walked and walked and walked and walked
til the sidewalk dissolved under her feet   her steps   thump thump thump   on soft earth

thump thump thump   thump thump thump   thump thump thump   thump thump thump
til crowgirl found herself in a clearing deep in the woods

crowgirl's legs feet were tired   her lungs working overtime
she stopped in that clearing   laid on her back
sinking into the soft earth   smiled   "done with it" she thought

takwâkin   autumn   a bed of dried leaves rested between crowgirl and askîy   earth
she let out a deep breath   looking up at kîsik   sky
it was a beautiful warm fall day   kîsik   was bright blue
the occasional cloud floating by   waving to crowgirl and all the beings around
another deep breath , a smile spread across crowgirl's face

quiet

this is the first quiet she'd heard in sooooooo long
soooooooooooooooooooooooooo   looooooooonnnnnnnnnnnnnnnnnng !

she breathed in the quiet   she heard the orchestra of beings crescendooOOOOOOO
plants breathing   shedding   prepping for   pipon   winter
rocks resting   smiling   warming in the gentle autumn sunshine
insects and animals   scurrying   collecting   insulating   storing for the cold
birds   all kinds   singing   talking   squawking   ... cawing!
"CAWING?!!"   crowgirl thoughtpanicked to herself   realizing crow was still there
"ughhhhhhhhhhh!!" she groaned   she thought she'd lost that pesky crow

swoooosh   swoooosh   swoooosh   wings flapping
cRunCh cruNch   leaves crunching   at her feet

crowgirl sat up

"Crow!"   she was surprised   that Crow had landed right in front of her
crowgirl realized she had never looked directly at Crow   this was the first time
Crow tilted its head   blinked its eyes   opened its beak
"tan'si!   how are you?"
crowgirl was stunned   Crow was speaking to her   in languages she could understand!
"uhhhhh . . . good? I guess??"   she stunnedreplied

Crow smiled   "ha! Sorry—didn't mean to catch you off guard"   Crow winked
"figured I've been around long enough you wouldn't be so startled!"   Crow chuckled

crowgirl chuckled   then chucklelaughed more   then laughter   **laughter!**   Pouring out of her
laugh laugh laugh laugh laugh laugh laugh laugh laugh
crowgirl felt the earth laughing underneath her
the plants around her the rocks insects animals birds
hahahahahaHAhaHaHahahaHAHAHAhahahAhAhAhahaHaHAHA
lololololololololololololololololololololololololololololololololololol

fear   distress   anxiety   despair   suicide   loneliness   hurt   pain   pouring out of her
askîy   plants   rocks   insects   animals   birds   breathing   transforming   creating
hahahahahaHAhaHaHahahaHAHAHAhahahAhAhAhahaHaHAHA
lololololololololololololololololololololololololololololololololololol

everyone was laughing so hard   gigglefit   sorestomach   tearsoflaughter
lololololololol
that laughing orchestra continued for ages it seemed   til   decrescendooooooooooo
trailing off   Iskotew wiped those   tearsoflaughter   from her eyes

Crow smiled   hopped from the leaves onto Iskotew's cross-legged knee
"geez ayyyyyyye girl! I've just been tryinna talk to you!"

those last few giggles escaped Iskotew's lips   "oy! Is that why you been so noisy?!"
"well chyaaaaa!! what   you think I've got time to harass young ladies for the heckuvit?"
Crow smiled   "everything has purpose you know   even a noisy crow" Crow winked
Iskotew smiled   a few more halfgiggles escaped   she'd heard that before   more than once
'everything has a purpose'

TEACHER GUIDE FOR APRIL RAINTREE AND IN SEARCH OF APRIL RAINTREE © 2024 CHRISTINE M'LOT © 2024 DR. KARLEE D. FELLNER (WELLNESS ACTIVITIES) ISBN: 978-1-77492-094-7

"actually that's what I been tryinna talk to you about Iskotew"
Iskotew looked around the whole forest was listening
but waitasec they weren't listening to Crow
they were listening to see if Iskotew was listening

"I been tryinna tell you your assistance is needed"
"huh?" Iskotew looked at Crow confused

"yep the two-leggeds are living in imbalance somewhere between the concrete slotmachines smartphones chemicals y'all seem to have lost your way forgot how to listen......... ahem! ... CLEARLY" Crow smilewinked at Iskotew "but not to worry that's why I'm here that's why we're here" Crow gestured to all the relatives around "we can see y'all are getting sick and tired of being sick and tired and heck we're sick and tired of it too"
the earthplantsrocksinsectsanimalsbirdsskyuniverse nodded in agreement

Iskotew let out a big sigh Crow was right she was sick and tired of being sick and tired
most people she knew were sick and tired of being sick and tired too
Iskotew shook her head
Crow hopped onto Iskotew's wrist "not to worry not like I squawked all this way just to leave you to find your way out on your own we can help y'all find your way back"
Iskotew perked up smiled "oh yeah?"
"of course! where you think your original instructions came from in the first place?"
Crow winked

Crow waved its wing over Iskotew's left hand "here"
Crow gave her 7 small grains of tobacco

"take this use it to get the medicines you need take those medicines back to the people
share them generously openly in a good way with the instructions that come to you"

Crow gestured toward the tobacco "each grain is a teaching a value that is needed by your people at this time when you offer a grain you will learn its medicine and come to understand its teaching you'll know where and when..."

Crow paused smiled at Iskotew "... just make sure you LISTEN..." Crow chuckled
Iskotew smiled back "but I don't know ..."

wing up Crow stopped her shook its head

"nuh uh uh!   you DO know   you just forgot you know   just LISTEN   and let us know when you need us   we'll be around to help you find your way when you get lost again   others of your nation will help you too   still some real good listeners out there"   Crow winkgrinned

Iskotew was unsure of herself   gulp!   she swallowed that lump of unsure in her throat
Crow was totally sure   Iskotew knew she had to trust that totally sure Crow   she nodded

Crow smiled   winked   hopped around in a few circles and spread its wings   flew off

bush life as usual resumed
Iskotew let out a deep sigh
looked at the grains of tobacco in her hand
she lay back on the bed of leaves again   taking some time to rest before going back to the busy-ness of human life

Iskotew felt the heaviness of human troubles she'd been carrying slide off of her into askîy
all that weight of distress about Crow was gone too   laughed into the earthskyuniverse

Iskotew thoughtgiggled to herself   "that whole time   Crow was trying to help me
I tried everything in the books!   Guess the 'listening' strategy must be 'in press'..."

as the sun set   Iskotew   walkdanced   from the bush   back to those familiar sidewalks

light   optimistic   unafraid   determined
all Iskotew's senses were clear   she looked around her
everything seemed new   colourful   alive   vibrant   diverse

she noticed so much she had never noticed before
she noticed many others who were distressed by helpers trying to get their attention
a young man trying to kickpunch a nipping coyote off his ankle
an elderly woman swatting at a persistent raven

Iskotew realized what a pitiful state the two-leggeds were in
love for her people filled her heart   she stopped at a tree by the gas station parking lot
laid down that first grain of tobacco   love   sâkihitowin
she asked for help   original instructions   so the people may know how to listen again

COMPREHENSION QUESTIONS AND DISCUSSION PROMPTS

Goals of These Activities: Students will actively read chapters 5–7 by taking notes, bookmarking important passages, and asking questions as they read. Students will be able to summarize the plot and themes of *April Raintree/In Search of April Raintree*, analyze the characters and their experiences, and discuss the social and historical context of the novel. Finally, students will create a character collage, an activity designed to encourage them to delve deeper into the characters' traits, corresponding animal transformations, motivations, and relationships.

MATERIALS

- copies of the novel *April Raintree* or *In Search of April Raintree*
- close-reading materials (e.g., highlighters, sticky notes)
- Discussion Participation Scale reproducible from Unit 1 (page 30; one copy for each student)
- materials for creating a collage (e.g., paper, magazines, pencil crayons or markers, scissors, glue or tape; or computer, tablet, or personal device)

DURATION

1–2 Hours

THE LESSON

ACTIVATE: THINK/PAIR/SHARE

Before beginning the reading, have students work in pairs to summarize the events in chapters 1–4.

Ask the pairs to reflect on the following question:

- How have April and Cheryl demonstrated survivance so far in the novel?

Ask volunteers to share their answers with the larger group.

ACQUIRE: READ CHAPTERS 5–7

Assign students the task of individually reading chapters 5–7. Encourage students to take notes, mark important passages, and ask questions as they read.

Encourage students to mark passages where April or Cheryl demonstrate survivance, thinking about what animals they each transform into while experiencing trauma.

For a reminder about topics of animal survivance, refer back to the video "Transformation and Survivance" (9:06) in Unit 2, Lesson 1 (page 40).

APPLY: SMALL-GROUP DISCUSSIONS

Once students have read the chapters, give each student a copy of the Discussion Participation Scale reproducible (from Unit 1, page 30). Review the discussion behaviours that students should strive for under "Active Involvement." Remind students that they are to review their discussion skills at the end of this novel study and that they should keep this completed Discussion Participation Scale with the one they completed in Unit 1, so that they can track their progress and set goals for improvement.

Organize the class into small groups to discuss the events of the novel and analyze the characters and themes. Encourage students to share their thoughts and ideas and facilitate a respectful and inclusive discussion. Provide students with questions and prompts, and allow groups approximately 2–3 minutes to discuss each question before having one person from the group summarize their conversation for the whole class.

Sample discussion prompts include:

1. Share one of your marked passages with your group. What stood out to you in this section and why?
2. Discuss the theme of friendship in this section. Who does April consider her friends? If you were April, would you consider them your friends? Why or why not?

3. How does April respond to Cheryl's essays about Métis culture? Discuss the differences in identity formation for April and Cheryl.

4. In this section Cheryl shares some of her hopes and dreams related to her and April's parents. What are they? How does April respond to them?

5. Why do you think April doesn't want Cheryl to attend the Academy with her? How is this an example of internalized racism? (See the definition of *internalized racism* on page 18.)

6. Discuss how the child welfare system is failing April in this section.

7. Describe an example of survivance from this section. How does this relate to trauma wisdom? (Trauma wisdom is described in the video "Transformation and Survivance" (9:06) on page 40.)

8. Does anything in these chapters relate to your inquiry project question (or questions, if it has not been focused to one question yet)?

ASSESS, PART 1: DISCUSSION PARTICIPATION SCALE

After the group discussions, have students complete the Discussion Participation Scale to track their own engagement in the small-group discussions. Collect the completed Discussion Participation Scales for formative assessment and return. When evaluating completed Discussion Participation Scales, note that some students may have chosen to opt out of certain discussions due to the subject matter. Therefore, formative assessments should be evaluated based on thoughtfulness and honesty, rather than participation in discussions.

Remind students that they are practising their group discussion skills throughout this novel study and will complete a Discussion Participation Scale after each unit's discussion to track their progress and reflect on their developing skills. Have students retain their completed Discussion Participation Scales for use at the end of Unit 5.

ASSESS, PART 2: CHARACTER COLLAGE

Have students work individually to create a character collage, choosing a character from the novel and creating a visual representation of which animal that character transforms into using images, symbols, and key quotes drawn from chapters 1–7. Students may choose to complete this collage on paper or online.

Optional: Use the sample reproducible below to assess this assignment. Clearly indicate to students that this assignment will be submitted and assessed.

  ISBN: 978-1-77492-094-7

Name: ____________________ Date: ____________________

CHARACTER COLLAGE ASSESSMENT

Creativity and Originality /5

Created a visually unique representation of the character's transformation into an animal. Incorporated creative elements, such as imaginative use of images, symbols, and key quotes.

Visual Representation /4

Effectively portrayed the character's transformation into an animal through the visual elements of the collage.

Integration of Elements /3

Integrated images, symbols, and key quotes in a cohesive and meaningful way to enhance the representation of the character's transformation.

Craftsmanship and Presentation /3

Demonstrated attention to detail, neatness, and skill in creating the collage. Presented the collage in a visually appealing and organized manner.

Total Grade /15

FINDING RELIABLE SOURCES

Goals of These Activities: Students will investigate a variety of sources and learn to identify reliable sources when conducting research, while learning about the child welfare system in Canada.

MATERIALS

- computers or tablets with internet access
- Unit 2 Exit Slip reproducible (page 56; one for each student)

DURATION

1.5 Hours

  ISBN: 978-1-77492-094-7

THE LESSON

ACTIVATE: WHERE DO YOU GET YOUR NEWS FROM?

Begin the lesson by asking students:

- Where do you get your news from?

Solicit answers and record them on the board.

Facilitate a brief class discussion about the sources mentioned. Ask students to consider the reliability, bias, and credibility of these sources. Prompt them to reflect on whether they have ever encountered misinformation or biased information in the news they consume. Ask:

- How did you find out it was misinformation?
- Why might misinformation or biased information be harmful?

Next, introduce the topic of the child welfare system. Say:

- While the child welfare system in Canada was originally created to help all children in need, it has disproportionately affected Indigenous families. The child welfare system has a history of removing Indigenous children from their homes and placing them in non-Indigenous foster care. This has been done under the guise of "protecting" Indigenous children, but has resulted in widespread loss of family and community ties. The child welfare system has also been criticized for not providing sufficient support and resources to Indigenous families, while over-representing Indigenous children in care compared to non-Indigenous children. Some say this has perpetuated ongoing trauma and harm to Indigenous communities and families, much like the residential school system.[25]

Ask the class:

- Why is it important to ensure the news we are getting about topics such as the child welfare system is true and accurate?

ACQUIRE: CHARACTERISTICS OF RELIABLE SOURCES

Introduce the importance of evaluating sources for reliability and credibility. Explain that not all sources are created equal, and critical evaluation is necessary to ensure accurate and trustworthy information.

[25] Aboriginal Justice Implementation Commission, "Child Welfare."

ISBN: 978-1-77492-094-7

Discuss the criteria for evaluating sources, including author credibility, source reputation, accuracy of information, where the author got their information from, whether any voices or perspectives are missing (representation), bias, and comparability to other sources. Share with students the 5Ws.

5 W Questions (5Ws): This method focuses on thinking critically about sources by asking five questions to determine whether a given source is credible and reliable.

- Who is the author? (Authority)
- What is the factual basis of the content? (Accuracy and Representation)
- Where is the content from? (Publisher)
- Why does the source exist? (Purpose and Objectivity)
- How does this source compare to others? (Determining What's What)

Ask students if they can think of anything else that might make a source credible or non-credible. Record their answers on the board. Introduce students to fact-checking sites that can help assess accuracy, such as PolitiFact, at <**https://www.politifact.com**>.

Note: PolitiFact is a Pulitzer Prize-winning site run by editors and reporters from the *Tampa Bay Times*. It is a fact-checking website that "rates the accuracy of claims by elected officials and others who speak up in American politics." State-specific PolitiFact pages are run by news organizations that have partnered with the *Tampa Bay Times*.[26]

APPLY, PART 1: FACT-CHECKING EXERCISE

Organize the class into groups of three to five students. Have each group use PolitiFact (if possible) to assess the accuracy of both of the following articles, and then use the 5Ws to further analyze both articles to determine whether the news each one contains is credible or not.

- Elizabeth Lawrence, "Biden DOJ quietly removes child sex trafficking content from its website," *American Military News*, July 12, 2023, at <https://americanmilitarynews.com/2023/07/biden-doj-quietly-removes-child-sex-trafficking-content-from-its-website/>.
- Carolyn Morris, "A bitter truth: 30 years of child welfare data reveals systemic inequities, racism and harm," *U of T News*, March 20, 2023, at <https://www.utoronto.ca/news/bitter-truth-30-years-child-welfare-data-reveals-systemic-inequities-racism-and-harm>.

[26] "Real News/Fake News: Fact Checkers," Berkeley Library.

Alternatively, select two articles of your choice for this activity, one that is credible and one that is not credible, based on current events and class interest.

Once all groups have finished their analysis, discuss their conclusions as a class.

APPLY, PART 2: TYING IT ALL TOGETHER

Ask students:

- Why do you think it's important to be able to spot misinformation?

Discuss as a class. Then, ask:

- Where can we get our information from to ensure it is reliable?

Have students brainstorm answers.

Refer to the list of the class's research questions created in Unit 1. Inform students that for the upcoming inquiry project, they should get their information from published journals, reliable news sources, university websites, trustworthy organizations, government websites, and books from reliable publishers, as these sources are fact-checked and/or peer-reviewed before publication. Students should avoid using personal blog posts, social media posts, unreliable news sources, or Wikipedia as sources, as these can be created by anyone without any requirements for checking accuracy.

Have students work in their inquiry project groups to identify one reliable source each (one per student) that will help them answer their research questions. Remind students that this is a good opportunity to review their research question and revise it if desired. (For example, a student whose research question was on colonialism might, after this unit, choose to narrow their topic to focus on the impact of the child welfare system on Indigenous communities.)

ASSESS: EXIT SLIP

Explain to students that they will complete an Exit Slip to demonstrate their understanding of how to identify reliable sources and their ability to apply this understanding to their inquiry project. Hand out a copy of the Unit 2 Exit Slip reproducible to each student and have students complete their Exit Slips individually.

Students will hand in the Exit Slip at the end of class.

Name: ____________________ Date: ____________________

UNIT 2 EXIT SLIP

My research questions are/My research question is:____________________

____

One reliable source that will help me answer this question is:____________________

____

Title:____________________

____

Source author: ____________________

____

Source container (website, journal, or book where the source is found): ____________________

____

Date of publication: ____________________

____

Briefly explain why this is a reliable source, with reference to the 5Ws:

- Who is the author? (Authority)____________________
- What is the factual basis of the content? (Accuracy and Representation)____________________
- Where is the content from? (Publisher)____________________
- Why does the source exist? (Purpose and Objectivity)____________________

____

- How does this source compare to others? (Determining What's What)____________________

____

____

3

ADULTHOOD PART 1 (CHAPTERS 8–11)

UNIT OVERVIEW

Before reading chapters 8–11, students will participate in a wellness activity designed to help them understand identity and Indigeneity. Next, students will read chapters 8–11 of the novel, while answering comprehension questions and engaging in small-group discussions about the themes and topics in the novel and how they relate to the larger historical context. Finally, students will learn to spot misinformation and stereotyping and will apply that learning as they investigate their research questions.

 ISBN: 978-1-77492-094-7

"RELATIONALITY AND INDIGENEITY" WELLNESS ACTIVITY

Goals of These Activities: Before reading chapters 8–11, students will engage in an activity designed to support their wellness while reading and learning about difficult topics. The wellness activity in this section will be about relationality and Indigeneity.

INFORMATION FOR TEACHERS

In this lesson, the phrase *attempted genocide* will be used. *Attempted genocide* refers to the Canadian government's assimilation policies towards Indigenous Peoples throughout history including the residential school system, the imposition of European belief systems, the outlawing of Indigenous ceremonies and cultural practices, and later, the mass removal of children from their homes through the child welfare system. These policies fit within Article 2 of the United Nations Genocide Convention, which defines genocide as:

1. *A mental element*: the "intent to destroy, in whole or in part, a national, ethnical, racial or religious group, as such"; and
2. *A physical element*, which includes the following five acts, enumerated exhaustively:
    > Killing members of the group
    > Causing serious bodily or mental harm to members of the group
    > Deliberately inflicting on the group conditions of life calculated to bring about its physical destruction in whole or in part
    > Imposing measures intended to prevent births within the group
    > Forcibly transferring children of the group to another group[27]

[27] "Genocide," The United Nations Office on Genocide Prevention and the Responsibility to Protect.

 ISBN: 978-1-77492-094-7

MATERIALS

- paper and writing utensils
- internet access
- projector

DURATION

1 Hour

  ISBN: 978-1-77492-094-7

THE LESSON

ACTIVATE: RELATIONSHIP WEB

Inform the class that they will be exploring the concepts of *relationality* and *Indigeneity*. Begin the lesson by providing students with paper and having them draw a relationship web.

Have students begin by writing their own names at the centre of the web. Next, have them record the first layer of their relations—their close family and friends. Beyond that they will draw the communities they are part of and identify with (e.g., language, cultural, spiritual, sports, music, arts). Then, have them draw the nations that they are part of (countries they are connected to, Indigenous Nations, etc.). Finally, have them draw the natural world (earth, water, air, animals, plants, insects, etc.), and the wider universe (sun, moon, stars, unseen/metaphysical aspects, etc.).

Once students have completed their web, encourage them to take notice of the many relationships through which they form connections. Have them choose to either individually reflect on the experience of completing this activity or reflect with a partner.

ACQUIRE: "RELATIONALITY" VIDEO

Show Dr. Fellner's video "Relationality" (9:05) at <https://youtu.be/xzdj7YFGb9g>, where she describes the connection between *relationality* and *Indigeneity* while discussing examples of survivance that Indigenous Peoples have used to combat attempted genocide.

As they watch, ask students to reflect on how their identities might shift and change based on the contexts and relationships they are in at the time (e.g., when they are with family or friends; when they are with a group of people and doing something they are really good at vs. something that is new to them).

APPLY: SURVIVANCE IN *APRIL RAINTREE/IN SEARCH OF APRIL RAINTREE*

Have students work in groups to debrief and reflect on what they've learned through Dr. Fellner's video and the activity of creating a relationship web. Then, have them find examples of relational survivance in chapters 1–7. The goal of this activity is to acknowledge the different ways people survive, and to honour all those ways (i.e., no one approach is "good" or "bad," "better" or "worse").

Have groups share their answers with each other.

ISBN: 978-1-77492-094-7

ASSESS/REFLECT: JOURNAL WRITING

Have students reflect on either of the following questions:

- How do the different aspects of who you are come out in different contexts (e.g., with family, with friends, out in public, with different groups of people)? Reflect on how this is part of your survivance and allows you to maintain harmonious relationships in those situations.
- You may also reflect on the relationships formed by characters in the novel, and explore how those relationships may bring out different aspects of who they are in different contexts. What are these examples, and how do they connect to the character's survivance?

Remind students that they do not have to share their entries with anyone, including you.

  ISBN: 978-1-77492-094-7

LESSON 2 DURING

COMPREHENSION QUESTIONS AND DISCUSSION PROMPTS

Goals of These Activities: Students will actively read chapters 8–11 by taking notes, marking important passages, and asking questions as they read. Students will be able to summarize the plot and themes of *April Raintree/In Search of April Raintree*, analyze the characters and their experiences, and discuss the social and historical context of the novel.

Content Warning: This section contains descriptions of sexual violence. Before assigning these chapters, you may wish to check your school or school board's protocols about the teaching of sensitive topics. You may also advise students which pages the descriptions appear on, if they wish to avoid them.

MATERIALS

- copies of the novel *April Raintree* or *In Search of April Raintree*
- close-reading materials (e.g., highlighters, sticky notes)
- Discussion Participation Scale reproducible from Unit 1 (page 30; one for each student)

DURATION

1–2 Hours

THE LESSON

ACTIVATE: QUOTE CATEGORIZATION

Begin the lesson by informing students that you are going to read them three quotes about resilience by three Indigenous women. Have students order the quotes from their favourite to least favourite, ensuring they can explain their reasoning. Encourage students to relate the quotes to Dr. Fellner's videos about survivance ("Transformation and Survivance" (9:06), Unit 2, Lesson 1, page 40), relationality ("Relationality" (9:05), Unit 3, Lesson 1, page 60), and healing from trauma ("Leaning Into the Land" (16:00), Unit 1, Lesson 1, page 23).

Use the following quotes, or select your own:

- "The land knows you, even when you are lost." From *Braiding Sweetgrass: Indigenous Wisdom, Scientific Knowledge, and the Teachings of Plants* (2013) by Robin Wall Kimmerer.
- "Find freedom in the context you inherit." From "Goodbye, Snauq" by Lee Maracle, Indigenous Canadian writer and academic of the Stó:lō Nation.
- "Strong communities are born out of individuals being their best selves." From *As We Have Always Done: Indigenous Freedom through Radical Resistance* (2017) by Leanne Betasamosake Simpson, Michi Saagiig Nishnaabeg scholar, writer, and artist.

Have students turn to a partner and discuss their respective lists, explaining the rationale behind choosing their favourite and least favourite quotes.

Before beginning the Unit 3 reading, have students work in pairs to summarize the events of chapters 5–7.

ACQUIRE: READ CHAPTERS 8–11

Assign students the task of individually reading chapters 8–11. Encourage students to take notes, mark important passages, and ask questions as they read.

APPLY: SMALL-GROUP DISCUSSIONS

Once students have read the chapters, give each student a copy of the Discussion Participation Scale reproducible (page 30). Review the discussion behaviours that students should strive for under "Active Involvement." Remind students that they are to review their discussion skills at the end of this novel study and that they should keep this completed Discussion Participation Scale with the ones they completed in the previous units so they can track their progress and set goals for improvement.

Organize the class into small groups to discuss the events of the novel and analyze the characters and themes. Encourage students to share their thoughts and ideas and facilitate a respectful and inclusive discussion. Provide students with questions and prompts, and allow groups approximately 2–3 minutes to discuss each question before having one person from the group summarize their conversation for the whole class.

Sample discussion prompts include:

1. Share one of your marked passages with your group. What stood out to you in this section and why?

2. What is April's reaction to visiting her parents' associate's home? How does this relate to her internalized racism?

3. How do you think Cheryl's relationship with Garth affected her? Why does Garth's treatment of Cheryl make April feel ashamed?

4. What are some examples of the racist treatment both April and Cheryl experience in this section?

5. How would you describe April and Bob's relationship?

6. What are some examples of the differences in survivance strategies between April and Cheryl in this section?

7. Discuss the end of this section. (Note that this discussion prompt may be optional.) What emotions were you feeling as you read? How did you cope with these emotions? What wellness activities would you recommend a person partake in if the content of these chapters is re-traumatizing?

8. Does anything in these chapters relate to your inquiry project question (or questions, if it has not been focused to one question yet)?

ASSESS, PART 1: DISCUSSION PARTICIPATION SCALE

After the group discussions, have students complete the Discussion Participation Scale to track their own engagement in the small-group discussions. Collect the completed Discussion Participation Scales for formative assessment and return. When evaluating completed Discussion Participation Scales, note that some students may have chosen to opt out of certain discussions due to the subject matter. Therefore, formative assessments should be evaluated based on thoughtfulness and honesty, rather than participation in discussions.

Remind students that they are practising their group discussion skills throughout this novel study and will complete a Discussion Participation Scale after each unit's discussion to track their progress and reflect on their developing skills. Have students retain their completed Discussion Participation Scales for use at the end of Unit 5.

ASSESS /REFLECT, PART 2: JOURNAL REFLECTION

Explain to students that they will be completing an independent journal entry to reflect on their understanding of survivance in the novel. (There is no reproducible for this activity.) Have each student write down a quote from the novel that they feel demonstrates April or Cheryl's survivance, with a short explanation of how the quote demonstrates survivance. They may choose to draw on personal experiences of survivance in order to explain their chosen quote, but it is not required.

Remind students that they do not have to show their journal reflection to anyone, including you.

CRITICAL LITERACY

Goals of These Activities: Throughout this activity students will learn to be critical of the sources they read and learn to spot stereotyping in media.

MATERIALS

- Unit 3 Exit Slip reproducible (page 69; one for each student)
- printed copies of four articles:
    - > “Ashamed of Your Pain? Overcoming Media Stereotypes About Trauma” at <https://michaelgquirke.com/ashamed-of-your-pain-overcoming-media-stereotypes-about-trauma/>.
    - > “Media Research: Movies’ PTSD Portrayal and Stereotypes” at <https://zeinafakhreddine.medium.com/media-research-movies-ptsd-portrayal-and-stereotypes-c01def6b1746>.
    - > “How the Stigma of Mental Health Is Spread by Mass Media” at <https://www.verywellmind.com/mental-health-stigmas-in-mass-media-4153888>.
    - > “The stigma that undermines care” at <https://www.apa.org/monitor/2019/06/cover-opioids-stigma>.

DURATION

1.5–2 Hours

THE LESSON

ACTIVATE: STEREOTYPES INTRODUCTION

Begin the lesson by asking if anyone knows what a *stereotype* is. Ask if anyone is willing to share the definition in their own words.

Explain that *stereotypes* are simplified and often exaggerated assumptions or beliefs about a particular group of people. For instance, one stereotype about Canadians is that all Canadians are polite. This is an example of a cultural stereotype. Then, point out that there are different *types* of stereotypes that students might encounter, including cultural, racial, and gender stereotypes.

Note: In order to avoid perpetuating stereotypes or hurting students in the class, it is important to avoid providing specific examples of racial, gender, or cultural stereotypes, and to avoid inviting students to offer specific examples. You might ask students to take a moment and silently think about stereotypes they have heard or seen, but explain that it is important not to repeat them, in order to keep the classroom a safe and respectful space.

Next, ask students why stereotypes are harmful. List their answers on the board.

ACQUIRE: ANALYZING STEREOTYPES IN MEDIA

Inform students that some topics covered in the news may contain or perpetuate harmful stereotypes. Explain that they are going to read some articles that will help them investigate some of the ways the media does this and how they can become critical readers and viewers.

Note: Although the first article is a blog post, it is written by a trained psychotherapist who is qualified to comment on the subject.

Have students work in their inquiry project groups. Hand out one article to each group. Inform the groups that their task is to read the article, summarize the main ideas, and report the findings to the rest of the class, while answering the following question:

- How can we become critical consumers of media?

Articles:

- "Ashamed of Your Pain? Overcoming Media Stereotypes About Trauma" at <https://michaelgquirke.com/ashamed-of-your-pain-overcoming-media-stereotypes-about-trauma/>.
- "Media Research: Movies' PTSD Portrayal and Stereotypes" at <https://zeinafakhreddine.medium.com/media-research-movies-ptsd-portrayal-and-stereotypes-c01def6b1746>.

- "How the Stigma of Mental Health Is Spread by Mass Media" at <https://www.verywellmind.com/mental-health-stigmas-in-mass-media-4153888>.
- "The stigma that undermines care" at <https://www.apa.org/monitor/2019/06/cover-opioids-stigma>.

Allow groups time to work.

Note: To extend student learning, have groups apply the 5Ws to the article they are working with, or discuss this as a class. To review the 5Ws, see Unit 2, Lesson 3: Acquire (page 54).

APPLY, PART 1: GROUP PRESENTATION ACTIVITY

Once groups have completed their analysis, have them take turns presenting their findings to the class, answering the question:

- How can we become critical consumers of media?

APPLY, PART 2: GROUP DISCUSSION

Once each group has presented their findings to the class, ask groups to discuss the final questions:

- How does analyzing stereotypes in sources contribute to critical thinking and media literacy?
- In what ways can you personally challenge and combat stereotypes in your media consumption and daily life?

Have groups review their research questions together and discuss whether they want to revise their research questions based on information from the articles. For example, a group interested in wellness might revise their question to focus on PTSD; a group interested in addiction and recovery might revise their question to focus on stigma and other barriers to recovery. Explain that they do not need to change their research questions; this is just an opportunity to revisit them.

ASSESS/REFLECT: EXIT SLIP

Remind students that they have already identified one source of information that will help their inquiry project (in the previous unit). Inform them that their group will need to identify three reliable sources in total. Either for homework or during class (make this decision based on your knowledge of your class's ability to conduct independent research), have students identify a second reliable source that contains information helpful to their inquiry project. Explain that they are welcome to choose one of the articles they examined as a class during this unit, but they do not have to. Give each student a copy of the Unit 3 Exit Slip reproducible (page 69) and have students complete and submit the Exit Slip individually. At this point it is not required that the entire group agrees which three reliable sources to focus on.

Name: ______________________ Date: ______________________

UNIT 3 EXIT SLIP

My research questions are/My research question is:______________________

____

A second reliable source that will help my group answer this question is:______________________

____

Title:______________________

____

Source author: ______________________

____

Source container (website, journal, or book where the source is found): ______________________

____

Date of publication: ______________________

____

Briefly explain why this is a reliable source, with reference to the 5Ws:_

- Who is the author? (Authority)______________________
- What is the factual basis of the content? (Accuracy and Representation)______________________
- Where is the content from? (Publisher)______________________
- Why does the source exist? (Purpose and Objectivity)______________________

____

- How does this source compare to others? (Determining What's What)______________________

____

____

 ISBN: 978-1-77492-094-7

4

ADULTHOOD PART 2 (CHAPTERS 12–15)

UNIT OVERVIEW

Before reading chapters 12–15, students will participate in a wellness activity designed to help them understand and reflect on the concept of *resistance*. Next, students will read chapters 12–15 of the novel, while answering comprehension questions and engaging in small-group discussions about the themes and topics in the novel and how they relate to the larger historical context. Finally, students will learn how to navigate and gather information from a variety of sources and will apply that learning as they investigate their research questions.

ISBN: 978-1-77492-094-7

"PROTECTION AND SURVIVANCE" WELLNESS ACTIVITY

Goals of These Activities: Before reading chapters 12–15, students will engage in an activity designed to support their wellness while reading and learning about difficult topics. In this wellness activity, students will learn about the concepts of protection and survivance in order to grow their knowledge on survivance, and continue to identify where it occurs throughout the novel.

MATERIALS

- internet access
- projector
- paper
- art supplies (e.g., drawing paper, markers, paints, paintbrushes, pencil crayons)

DURATION

1.5–2 Hours

THE LESSON

ACTIVATE: SURVIVANCE BRAINSTORM

Begin the lesson by having students individually think about the ways they've used survivance when dealing with a difficult person or situation in the past (e.g., bullying, oppression, infringement on their rights) or the way someone else they know has done so. This might include withdrawing from the situation, telling a trusted adult, asking for help, or other forms of survivance. Have students volunteer to share their answers with the class, or share some of your own examples. Record a list on the board for all to see.

ACQUIRE: "LAND-BASED TOOLS FOR SITTING WITH TRAUMA" VIDEO

Show Dr. Fellner's video "Land-Based Tools for Sitting With Trauma" (17:18) at <https://youtu.be/PDvvspv7UxE>. Students may wish to take notes as they watch the video to support their basic understanding of trauma responses and helpful tools that can be used when interacting with triggering content.

After the video, ask students to volunteer to share some of the land-based tools a person can use as they continue to read the book. These might be some strategies shared by Dr. Fellner, or strategies the students come up with or already use.

APPLY: ANIMAL HELPERS IN *APRIL RAINTREE/IN SEARCH OF APRIL RAINTREE*

Ask students to either reflect individually or turn to a partner and discuss the animal helpers that come up in *April Raintree/In Search of April Raintree*. In many Indigenous cultures, an animal helper is seen as a spirit guide or a source of inspiration, protection, and guidance. You may choose to have students watch the video "Transformation and Survivance" (9:06), from Unit 2, Lesson 1, on page 40. It explores the topic of animal transformation, which may support this discussion.

Allow students time to create an art piece to honour an animal protector in *April Raintree/In Search of April Raintree*, or in their own lives. Remind students to consider all the chapters they have read so far (1–11).

Allow students 45 minutes to work on their art piece.

ASSESS/REFLECT: JOURNAL REFLECTION

Have students create a journal entry answering the following question:

- How could someone use the knowledge and wisdom shared so far in these wellness lessons (e.g., leaning into the land, connect and protect, transformation, focus on survivance) when interacting with difficult subject matter, such as the descriptions and situations in the novel?

Remind students that they do not have to share their journal entry with anyone, including you.

COMPREHENSION QUESTIONS AND DISCUSSION PROMPTS

Goals of These Activities: Students will actively read chapters 12–15 by taking notes, marking important passages in the novel, and asking questions as they read. Students will be able to summarize the plot and themes of *April Raintree/In Search of April Raintree*, analyze the characters and their experiences, and discuss the social and historical context of the novel.

Content Warning: This section contains discussions of sexual violence. Before assigning these chapters, you may wish to check your school or school board's protocols about the teaching of sensitive topics. You may also advise students which pages the discussions appear on, if they wish to avoid them.

MATERIALS

- copies of the novel *April Raintree* or *In Search of April Raintree*
- close-reading materials (e.g., highlighters, sticky notes)
- Discussion Participation Scale reproducible from Unit 1 (page 30; one for each student)
- paper

DURATION

1–2 Hours

THE LESSON

ACTIVATE: WELLNESS RECALL GAME

Begin the lesson by informing students that they are going to play a recall game to enhance their recollection of the wellness lessons to date.

The Recall Game:

- Student A names a wellness word; for example, *survivance.*
- Student B must name a word that starts with the last letter of the previous student's word. For example, Student B must think of a wellness word that starts with E.
- The game continues until all students have had a chance to share a word.
- Students don't necessarily have to think of a wellness word explicitly taught in class—they can think of synonyms, or any other word that applies to wellness in their own lives or in the lives of others.

Before reading the next section, have students summarize the events of chapters 8–11 with a partner.

ACQUIRE: READ CHAPTERS 12–15

Assign students the task of individually reading chapters 12–15. Encourage students to take notes, mark important passages, and ask questions as they read.

APPLY: SMALL-GROUP DISCUSSIONS

Once students have read the chapters, give each student a copy of the Discussion Participation Scale reproducible (page 30). Review the discussion behaviours that students should strive for under "Active Involvement." Remind students that they are to review their discussion skills at the end of this novel study and that they should keep this completed Discussion Participation Scale with the ones they completed in the previous units, so that they can track their progress and set goals for improvement.

Organize the class into small groups to discuss the events of the novel and to analyze the characters and themes. Encourage students to share their thoughts and ideas and facilitate a respectful and inclusive discussion. Provide students with questions and prompts, and allow groups approximately 2–3 minutes to discuss each question before having one person from the group summarize their conversation for the whole class.

Sample discussion prompts include:

1. Share one of your marked passages with your group. What stood out to you in this section and why?
2. Describe how April is responding to the trauma she experienced. What is the role of water in her healing and how does this relate to her past?
3. Discuss the evolution of Cheryl's drinking problem. What clues does April notice that Cheryl may have an addiction?
4. Is Roger a good support for April? Justify your answer by citing evidence from the text.
5. How did attending the powwow affect April and Cheryl?
6. How does April and Cheryl's relationship change in this section?
7. Describe some examples of survivance and resilience in this section.
8. Does anything in these chapters relate to your inquiry project question (or questions, if it has not been focused to one question yet)?

ASSESS, PART 1: DISCUSSION PARTICIPATION SCALE

After the group discussions, have students complete the Discussion Participation Scale to track their own engagement in the small-group discussions. Collect the completed Discussion Participation Scales for formative assessment and return. When evaluating completed Discussion Participation Scales, note that some students may have chosen to opt out of certain discussions due to the subject matter. Therefore, formative assessments should be evaluated based on thoughtfulness and honesty, rather than participation in discussions.

Remind students that they are practising their group discussion skills throughout this novel study and will complete a Discussion Participation Scale after each unit's discussion to track their progress and reflect on their developing skills. Have students retain their completed Discussion Participation Scales for use at the end of Unit 5.

ASSESS, PART 2: FREE WRITE

Turn students' attention to Cheryl's essay. Allow students time to review the essay individually, or read it together as a class.

Provide students with writing paper and inform them that they will be given 10 minutes to write about their thoughts, emotions, connections, and/or questions about Cheryl's essay through a free-write task.

Have students submit their free write at the end of class.

Use the free-write assignment as a form of formative assessment to gauge how well students grasped the key points of Cheryl's essay. The assignment may also provide valuable feedback that will help you tailor future lessons to address specific areas of confusion or reinforce important concepts.

  ISBN: 978-1-77492-094-7

NAVIGATING AND GATHERING INFORMATION FROM SOURCES

Goals of These Activities: Students will learn to navigate and gather information from sources.

MATERIALS

- internet access
- computers or tablets
- research materials (e.g., books, articles, videos)
- Navigating Sources reproducible (page 80; one for each student)
- Unit 4 Exit Slip reproducible (page 79; one for each student)

DURATION

1 Hour

THE LESSON

ACTIVATE: ADDICTION DEFINITION

To begin the lesson, introduce the topic of addiction to the class. Say:

- Addiction is a treatable condition involving complex interactions among brain circuits, genetics, the environment, and an individual's life experiences.[28] Addiction offers temporary relief from pain (physical, emotional, mental, and/or spiritual), and gives an individual a short-term sense of control and calmness. In the long term, addiction has many negative consequences; however, it is very difficult for the person experiencing the addiction to give it up, despite the consequences.[29]

Inform the class that learning about addiction will help them understand Cheryl's response to trauma.

ACQUIRE: NAVIGATING SOURCES

Inform students that today they will be practising the skill of navigating sources. This is an important skill because sometimes the sources that we use will be information-dense, which might lead us to become overwhelmed. By learning to navigate a variety of sources, we can ensure we know where to look for specific pieces of information.

Explain that students are going to be given a list of sources they can use to help them answer various research questions. For this activity, all students will research the following question:

- "What causes addiction?"

However, the materials explored here might also be of use to groups researching many different topics, such as stigma, wellness, recovery, or relationships. Resource examples include:

- The Centre for Addiction and Mental Health (CAMH): CAMH is a leading Canadian research organization for mental health and addiction. They provide information and resources on addiction and its effects, including support for those who are struggling with addiction. https://www.camh.ca
- Drug Free Kids Canada (DFKC): DFKC is a non-profit organization that provides information and resources on substance use and addiction, including educational materials and prevention strategies. https://www.drugfreekidscanada.org

---

[28] "Definition of Addiction," American Society of Addiction Medicine.

[29] "The Power of Addiction and the Addiction to Power | Gabor Maté, MD," *Mad in America: Science, Psychiatry and Social Justice.*

- Canadian Centre on Substance Use and Addiction (CCSA): CCSA was created through an act of Parliament in 1988 to develop a strategic plan toward fostering understanding and creating awareness of substance-use issues by creating accessible, evidence-informed publications. https://ccsa.ca

- Dr. Gabor Maté: Dr. Gabor Maté is a Canadian physician, author, and public speaker. After working for 20 years in family practice and palliative care, he now shares insights into complex physical, emotional, and spiritual issues by weaving together scientific research, case studies, and his own experiences. His website provides further information into topics such as addiction, mental and physical health, and trauma. https://drgabormate.com/

APPLY: NAVIGATING SOURCES

Provide students with the Navigating Sources reproducible (page 80). Have students browse their sources and complete the worksheet individually.

Give students 45 minutes to complete this activity.

Once students complete the activity, have them review their answers in their inquiry project groups. Ask:

- Did anyone in the group find any relevant information other members missed? How so?

- What tips did each of you use to navigate the various websites?

ASSESS: EXIT SLIP

Explain to students that they will complete an Exit Slip to demonstrate their understanding of how to navigate various websites and assess the information they provide. Give each student a copy of the Unit 4 Exit Slip reproducible. Have students complete and submit the Exit Slips individually.

Name: ______________________ Date: ______________________

UNIT 4 EXIT SLIP

My research questions are/My research question is:______________________

____

The website and section that I found most useful for answering my research question is:

____

____

Title:______________________

____

Source author: ______________________

____

Navigation (website, page, heading, tab): ______________________

____

Briefly explain why this webpage or section is especially useful to your inquiry project:

____

____

____

____

____

____

____

____

____

Name: ____________________ Date: ____________________

NAVIGATING SOURCES

Review the following websites, navigating to the relevant pages and sections that help answer the research question:

- What causes addiction?

Resource	Navigation—Which pages, headings, and tabs were most relevant?	What specific information can you find in the relevant section(s) that helps answer the research question?	What specific information, if any, can you find that helps answer your own research question?
The Centre for Addiction and Mental Health (CAMH): CAMH is a leading Canadian research organization for mental health and addiction. They provide information and resources on addiction and its effects, including support for those who are struggling with addiction. https://www.camh.ca			
Drug Free Kids Canada (DFKC): DFKC is a non-profit organization that provides information and resources on substance use and addiction, including educational materials and prevention strategies. https://www.drugfreekidscanada.org			

4.3.2

Name: ______________________ Date: ______________________

Canadian Centre on Substance Use and Addiction (CCSA): CCSA was created through an act of Parliament in 1988 to develop a strategic plan toward fostering understanding and creating awareness of substance-use issues by creating accessible, evidence-informed publications. https://ccsa.ca			
Dr. Gabor Maté: Dr. Gabor Maté is a Canadian physician, author, and public speaker. After working for 20 years in family practice and palliative care, he now shares insights into complex physical, emotional, and spiritual issues by weaving together scientific research, case studies, and his own experiences. His website provides further information into topics such as addiction, mental and physical health, and trauma. https://drgabormate.com			

  ISBN: 978-1-77492-094-7

5

LEGACY (CHAPTERS 16–17)

UNIT OVERVIEW

Before reading chapters 16–17, students will participate in a wellness activity designed to help them understand and reflect on the topics of grief and transformation. Next, students will read chapters 16–17, while answering comprehension questions and engaging in small-group discussions about the themes and topics in the novel and how they relate to the larger historical context. Finally, students will learn what makes a great presentation and will apply that learning in a group presentation on their completed inquiry projects.

ISBN: 978-1-77492-094-7

"TRANSFORMATION" WELLNESS ACTIVITY

Goals of These Activities: Before reading chapters 16–17, students will engage in an activity designed to support their wellness while reading and learning about difficult topics. In this culminating activity, students will learn about grief and transformation while creating art.

MATERIALS

- art supplies (e.g., drawing paper, markers, paints, paintbrushes, pencil crayons)
- internet access
- computers or tablets

DURATION

2 Hours

THE LESSON

ACTIVATE: EXPLORING THE CONCEPT OF GRIEF

To begin the lesson, give students a sheet of drawing paper (unlined) and invite them to jot down anything that comes to mind when they think about grief (or about healing from grief). They can write their own thoughts, draw pictures, or record quotes from songs or elsewhere.

Allow students 15–20 minutes to complete this.

ACQUIRE: "GRIEF AND SUICIDE" VIDEO

Next, show the class Dr. Fellner's video "Grief and Suicide" (23:20) at <https://youtu.be/vzcImYFedIw>, in which she shares Indigenous understandings of grief and suicide.

APPLY: MEDICINE ART

Explain to students that, on the other side of their jotting about grief, they will create art. The purpose of the art is to transform that grief into medicine. Each student should choose one of the following topics. (Consider giving students the option of creating a handmade collage or a digital collage.)

- Create a collage (this can include words as well as images) of all the medicines that can help us deal with grief (e.g., land, water, sunlight, flowers, loved ones, nourishment).
- Create a collage of some things you enjoy or feel positively about. If appropriate, you may choose to let students know that they may return to this collage (or something else in their life that inspires happiness) as a jumping-off point if they are feeling down or uninspired.

Give students about one hour to complete their collage. If appropriate, share that students may return to these collages as they or others in their lives move through periods of grief and transformation.

COMPREHENSION QUESTIONS AND DISCUSSION PROMPTS

Goals of These Activities: Students will actively read chapters 16–17 by taking notes, marking important passages in the novel, and asking questions as they read. Students will be able to summarize the plot and themes of *April Raintree/In Search of April Raintree*, analyze the characters and their experiences, and discuss the social and historical context of the novel.

MATERIALS

- copies of the novel *April Raintree* or *In Search of April Raintree*
- close-reading materials (e.g., highlighters, sticky notes)
- Discussion Participation Scale reproducible from Unit 1 (page 30; one for each student)

DURATION

1–2 Hours

THE LESSON

ACTIVATE: GRIEF MEDICINE ART GALLERY WALK

Give students the option to showcase their collages from the previous lesson to the class. Display the art around the class, encouraging students to walk around the room and look at each piece. Allow students 15 minutes for the activity.

You may also showcase grief artwork by Indigenous artists and review related articles, videos, and essays, such as:

- "First Nations artists process grief from Kamloops residential school discovery through their work," at <https://www.cbc.ca/news/indigenous/artists-kamloops-residential-school-1.6048984>.
- "Art Connects | On Collective Grief," at <https://www.vanartgallery.bc.ca/events/art-connects-on-collective-grief>.
- "Moving through Grief," at <https://canadianart.ca/essays/art-and-grief/>.

Ask:

- What do you notice about the art displayed? This could include the differences in artistic mediums, such as collage or paint. How can this inform us about the many ways strength and survivance can be portrayed?

ACQUIRE: READ CHAPTERS 16–17

Assign students the task of individually reading chapters 16–17. Encourage students to take notes, mark important passages, and ask questions as they read.

APPLY: SMALL-GROUP DISCUSSIONS

Once students have read the chapters, give each student a copy of the Discussion Participation Scale reproducible (page 30). Review the discussion behaviours that students should strive for under "Active Involvement." Remind students that they are to review their discussion skills at the end of this novel study and that they should keep this completed Discussion Participation Scale with the ones they completed in previous units so that they can track their progress.

Organize the class into small groups to discuss the events of the novel and analyze the characters and themes. Encourage students to share their thoughts and ideas and facilitate a respectful and inclusive discussion. Provide students with questions and prompts, and allow groups approximately 2–3 minutes to discuss each question before having one person from the group summarize their conversation for the whole class.

Sample discussion prompts may include:

1. Share one of your marked passages with your group. What stood out to you in this section and why?
2. What do Cheryl's letters reveal?
3. How did Cheryl cope with her trauma?
4. Discuss the concept of guilt and how it comes up in this section.
5. What does April promise at the end?
6. How do the themes of survivance and transformation appear in both Cheryl's and April's lives?
7. What do you think the author's purpose for writing this story was?
8. Does anything in these chapters relate to your inquiry project question?

After the group discussions, have students each complete the Discussion Participation Scale reproducible (page 30) to track their engagement in the small-group discussions. Collect the completed Discussion Participation Scales for formative assessment and return. When evaluating completed Discussion Participation Scales, note that some students may have chosen to opt out of certain discussions due to the subject matter. Therefore, formative assessments should be evaluated based on thoughtfulness and honesty, rather than participation in discussions.

ASSESS DISCUSSION SKILLS

Have students review their completed Discussion Participation Scales from all five units. For homework, have students compose and submit a written reflection (half a page to one page in length) on how their participation skills changed and improved throughout the novel study.

ASSESS COMPREHENSION: APRIL'S LEGACY COLLAGE

Have students take on the role of April and create a collage based on her experiences throughout the novel. The idea of this collage should be to convey April's hopes for the future in a way that shows the joy that inspires hope in her life. Have students reflect on how the collage is similar to and different from the collage they created in Lesson 1.

LESSON 3 AFTER

PRESENTATION SKILLS AND FINAL INQUIRY PROJECT

Goals of These Activities: Students will watch a presentation about Indigenous perspectives on wellness while noticing what makes a great presentation. Then, students will begin their final inquiry project into a subtopic of their choice.

MATERIALS

- chart paper and markers
- internet access
- projector
- computers or tablets
- Inquiry Project Research reproducible (pages 91–92; one for each student)
- Inquiry Project Assessment Rubric reproducible (page 93)

DURATION

4 Hours (Activate and Acquire: 1 Hour; research and creating presentations: 2 Hours; presentations: 1 Hour)

THE LESSON

ACTIVATE: RESEARCH QUESTION REVIEW DISCUSSION

To begin the lesson, display the list of research questions compiled in Unit 1. Have students share whether their inquiry project group's question has changed over the past few units and why. Remind students that they have already identified two reliable sources (in Units 2 and 3) and may have identified one or more in Unit 4. Next, have students share what they remember from previous units about what makes a reliable source (Unit 2), how to critically evaluate a source (Unit 3), and how to navigate and gather information from online sources (Unit 4).

ACQUIRE: TED TALK

Show students the video of Cohen Bradley's Ted Talk "How to Weave a Cultural Legacy Through Storytelling" (10:13), encouraging students to notice the presentation skills of the presenter.

Video: <**https://www.ted.com/talks/cohen_bradley_how_to_weave_a_cultural_legacy_through_storytelling**>.

Debrief the video. Ask:

- How does this video relate to the novel study, and to the concept of survivance more specifically?

Then discuss the speaker's presentation in the video. Ask:

- What made this a great presentation?

Record the answers on the board, so students can recall the characteristics of a good presentation before their final presentation date.

APPLY: COMPLETE AND PRESENT THE INQUIRY PROJECTS

Remind students that they need to include information gathered from three reliable sources in their presentation. Project the Inquiry Project Assessment Rubric and discuss the criteria for a successful presentation with the class. Next, give each student a copy of the Inquiry Project Research reproducible (pages 91–92) and give students 30–40 minutes to ensure that they have three reliable sources and to begin recording the information they find. Have students complete these forms for homework. Depending on your teaching goals and your knowledge of your class's experience with creating research presentations, allow groups one or two classes to create a short presentation (10 minutes maximum) to share the answer to their research question, or assign the presentation preparation as homework.

Have groups make their presentations to the class.

ASSESS: INQUIRY PROJECT ASSESSMENT

Assess students individually on their group presentations, using the Inquiry Project Assessment Rubric on page 93.

Name: ______________________ Date: ______________________

INQUIRY PROJECT RESEARCH

My research question:____

____

SOURCE #1

Title:____

____

Source author: ____

____

Source container (website, journal, or book where the source is found): ______________

____

Date of publication: ____

____

Information that helps you answer your research question (point form is fine):

____

____

____

____

____

____

____

____

SOURCE #2

Title: ______________________________

Source author: ______________________________

Source container (website, journal, or book where the source is found): ______________________________

____

Date of publication: ______________________________

Summarize your learning here: ______________________________

____

____

____

____

SOURCE #3

Title: ______________________________

Source author: ______________________________

Source container (website, journal, or book where the source is found): ______________________________

____

Date of publication: ______________________________

Summarize your learning here: ______________________________

____

____

____

____

Name: ______________________ Date: ______________________

INQUIRY PROJECT ASSESSMENT RUBRIC

	Needs Improvement 0–5 marks	Good 6–9 marks	Excellent 10 marks
Quality of Research Question	The question is vague, unclear, or lacks specificity, making it difficult to understand, or is unrelated to the topic.	The question is somewhat clear but may lack precision, relevance, or depth of thought.	The question is clear, concise, specific, relevant to the topic, and demonstrates depth of thought.
Knowledge of the Topic	The student's understanding of the topic is limited, inaccurate, or contains significant misconceptions or stereotypes.	The student shows some familiarity with the topic but some information may contain inaccuracies or misconceptions.	The student demonstrates a deep understanding of the topic, with accuracy and precision.
Quality of Sources	The sources used are unreliable, irrelevant, or insufficient to support the research topic.	The sources used are somewhat relevant and credible but may lack depth or variety.	The sources used are highly relevant, credible, and provide comprehensive support for the research topic.
Presentation Skills	The presentation lacks organization, clarity, and engagement; the presenter is distracted or unprepared at times.	The presentation is somewhat organized, clear, and engaging, but needs improvement in one or more aspects.	The presentation is well-organized, clear, engaging, and effectively conveys the project's content.

Teacher's Comments:

/40

RESOURCES FOR TEACHERS AND STUDENTS

BOOKS AND ARTICLES

Benn, Carl. *Mohawks on the Nile: Natives Among the Canadian Voyageurs in Egypt, 1884–1885*. Toronto: Dundurn Press, 2009.

Fellner, Karlee D. "Iskotew & Crow: Reigniting Narratives of Indigenous Survivance and Trauma Wisdom in the Classroom." In *Knowing the Past, Facing the Future: Indigenous Education in Canada*, edited by S. Carr-Stewart, and J. Ottmann, 143–170. Vancouver: UBC Press, 2019.

Fellner, K. D., R. John, and S. Cottell. "Counselling Indigenous peoples in a Canadian context." In *Handbook of Counselling and Psychotherapy in Canada*, edited by N. Gazzola, M. Buchanan, O. Sutherland, and S. Nuttgens, 123–147. Ottawa: Canadian Counselling and Psychotherapy Association, 2016.

Katz, Jennifer, with Kevin Lamoureux. *Ensouling Our Schools: A Universally Designed Framework for Mental Health, Well-Being, and Reconciliation*. Winnipeg: Portage & Main Press, 2018.

Kimmerer, Robin Wall. *Braiding Sweetgrass: Indigenous Wisdom, Scientific Knowledge and the Teaching of Plants*. Minneapolis: Milkweed Editions, 2013.

Vizenor, Gerald. *Manifest Manners: Narratives on Postindian Survivance*. Lincoln: University of Nebraska Press, 1999.

ONLINE RESOURCES

Aboriginal Justice Implementation Commission. "Child Welfare." *The Justice System and Aboriginal People*. Winnipeg: Government of Manitoba, 1991. http://www.ajic.mb.ca/volumel/chapter14.html.

Bradley, Cohen. "How to weave a cultural legacy through storytelling." Ted@DestinationCanada, February 2023. https://www.ted.com/talks/cohen_bradley_how_to_weave_a_cultural_legacy_through_storytelling.

Butler, Lisa D., Filomena M. Critelli, and Elaine S. Rinfrette. "Trauma-Informed Care and Mental Health." *Directions in Psychiatry* 31 (January 2011): 177–192. https://www.researchgate.net/profile/Lisa-Butler-5/publication/234155324_Trauma-Informed_Care_and_Mental_Health/.

Carleton, Sean. "John A. Macdonald was the real architect of residential schools." *Toronto Star*, July 9, 2017. https://www.thestar.com/opinion/contributors/john-a-macdonald-was-the-real-architect-of-residential-schools/article_8b82cccc-9a5f-5c6d-864a-0241ddf63335.html.

"Chapter 1: Terminology." *Indigenous Voices Online Learning Modules: Power and Privilege*. University of Saskatchewan. https://teaching.usask.ca/curriculum/indigenous_voices/power-and-privilege/chapter-1.php.

"Citizenship Application–FAQ's." Manitoba Métis Federation. https://www.mmf.mb.ca/citizenship-application-faqs.

"Definition of Addiction." American Society of Addiction Medicine, September 15, 2019. https://www.asam.org/quality-care/definition-of-addiction.

"Did You Live Near a Residential School?" CBC News, 2017. https://www.cbc.ca/news2/interactives/beyond-94-residential-school-map/.

Fakhreddine, Zeina, Eman Chaiban, Dana Ghanem, and Tanya Ghawi. "Media Research: Movies' PTSD Portrayal and Stereotypes." Medium.com, January 17, 2017. https://zeinafakhreddine.medium.com/media-research-movies-ptsd-portrayal-and-stereotypes-c01def6b1746.

"First Nations in Canada." Crown-Indigenous Relations and Northern Affairs Canada. Updated May 2, 2017. https://www.rcaanc-cirnac.gc.ca/eng/1307460755710/1536862806124.

"Genocide." The United Nations Office on Genocide Prevention and the Responsibility to Protect. https://www.un.org/en/genocideprevention/genocide.shtml.

Greenbaum, Zara. "The stigma that undermines care." *Monitor on Psychology* 50, no. 6 (June 2019). American Psychological Association. https://www.apa.org/monitor/2019/06/cover-opioids-stigma.

"Grief." *Psychology Topics*. American Psychological Association. https://www.apa.org/topics/grief.

"Indigenous Peoples and Communities." Crown-Indigenous Relations and Northern Affairs Canada. Updated August 30, 2022. https://www.rcaanc-cirnac.gc.ca/eng/1100100013785/1529102490303#.

"iskotew & crow: (re)igniting narratives of Indigenous survivance & trauma w/ Dr. Karlee Fellner." Simon Fraser University Department of Psychology, May 17, 2022. https://www.youtube.com/watch?v=47oj13edpSo.

Johnson, Rhiannon. "First Nations artists process grief from Kamloops residential school discovery through their work." *CBC*, June 2, 2021. https://www.cbc.ca/news/indigenous/artists-kamloops-residential-school-1.6048984.

Korducki, Kelli. "Moving through Grief." *canadianart*, February 6, 2018. https://canadianart.ca/essays/art-and-grief/.

Lackenbauer, Whitney P., John Moses, R. Scott Sheffield, and Maxime Gohier. "The Arrival of the Europeans: 17th Century Wars." In *A Commemorative History of Aboriginal People in the Canadian Military*. Ottawa: Department of National Defence, 2018. Government of Canada. https://www.canada.ca/en/department-national-defence/services/military-history/history-heritage/popular-books/aboriginal-people-canadian-military/arrival-europeans-17th-century-wars.html.

Lawrence, Elizabeth. "Biden DOJ quietly removes child sex trafficking content from its website." *American Military News*, July 12, 2023. https://americanmilitarynews.com/2023/07/biden-doj-quietly-removes-child-sex-trafficking-content-from-its-website/.

Manitoba Education and Youth. *Integrating Aboriginal Perspectives Into Curricula*. Manitoba Education and Early Childhood Learning. Winnipeg: Government of Manitoba, 2003. https://www.edu.gov.mb.ca/k12/docs/policy/abpersp/ab_persp.pdf.

"Métis Identity." *Indigenous Peoples Atlas of Canada*. Canadian Geographic. https://indigenouspeoplesatlasofcanada.ca/article/identity/.

Métis Minute. Manitoba Métis Federation. https://www.mmf.mb.ca/metis-minute.

Miller, James R., with updates by Zach Parrott. "Indigenous-British Relations Pre-Confederation." *Canadian Encyclopedia*, February 7, 2006; updated May 26, 2015. https://www.thecanadianencyclopedia.ca/en/article/aboriginal-european-relations.

Miller, J. R., with updates by Tabitha De Bruin, David Gallant, and Michelle Filice. "Residential Schools in Canada." *Canadian Encyclopedia*, October 10, 2012; updated January 6, 2023. https://www.thecanadianencyclopedia.ca/en/article/residential-schools.

Morris, Carolyn. "A bitter truth: 30 years of child welfare data reveals systemic inequities, racism and harm." *U of T News*, March 20, 2023. https://www.utoronto.ca/news/bitter-truth-30-years-child-welfare-data-reveals-systemic-inequities-racism-and-harm.

The Indigenous Peoples Atlas of Canada. Canadian Geographic. https://indigenouspeoplesatlasofcanada.ca/.

PolitiFact. Poynter Institute. https://www.politifact.com.

"The Power of Addiction and the Addiction to Power | Gabor Maté, MD." *Mad in America: Science, Psychiatry and Social Justice*, March 23, 2022. https://www.madinamerica.com/2022/03/the-power-of-addiction-and-the-addiction-to-power-gabor-mate-md/.

Pyke, Karen D. "What is Internalized Racial Oppression and Why Don't We Study It? Acknowledging Racism's Hidden Injuries." *Sociological Perspectives* 53, no. 4 (December 2010): 551–572. https://doi.org/10.1525/sop.2010.53.4.551.

Quirke, Michael G. "Ashamed of Your Pain? Overcoming Media Stereotypes About Trauma." Michaelgquirke.com. https://michaelgquirke.com/ashamed-of-your-pain-overcoming-media-stereotypes-about-trauma/#.

"Real News/Fake News: Fact Checkers." Berkeley Library. Updated November 27, 2023. https://guides.lib.berkeley.edu/c.php?g=620677&p=4333407.

Reece, Skeena and Marcia Crosby. "Art Connects | On Collective Grief." Vancouver Art Gallery, June 20, 2022. https://www.vanartgallery.bc.ca/events/art-connects-on-collective-grief.

"The Residential School System." Parks Canada. Updated September 1, 2020. https://www.canada.ca/en/parks-canada/news/2020/09/the-residential-school-system.html#shr-pg0.

Roy, Dale, Erika Kustra, and Paola Borin. "What Is a 'Good' Inquiry Question?" McMaster University, 2003. https://cll.mcmaster.ca/resources/misc/good_inquiry_question.html

Royal Commission on Aboriginal Peoples. *Highlights From the Report of the Royal Commission on Aboriginal Peoples*. Government of Canada. Updated September 15, 2010. https://www.rcaanc-cirnac.gc.ca/eng/1100100014597/1572547985018.

Saleh, Naveed. "How the Stigma of Mental Health Is Spread by Mass Media." Verywell Mind. Updated January 16, 2023. https://www.verywellmind.com/mental-health-stigmas-in-mass-media-4153888.

"Trauma." *Psychology Topics*. American Psychological Association. https://www.apa.org/topics/trauma.

"What is Posttraumatic Stress Disorder (PTSD)?" American Psychiatric Association, November 2022. https://www.psychiatry.org/patients-families/ptsd/what-is-ptsd.

SUPPORT RESOURCES FOR YOUTH AND FAMILY

Alcoholics Anonymous (AA)
https://www.aa.org

Canadian Centre on Substance Use and Addiction (CCSA)
https://ccsa.ca

The Canadian Mental Health Association (CMHA)
https://cmha.ca

Canadian Virtual Hospice
https://www.virtualhospice.ca

The Centre for Addiction and Mental Health (CAMH)
https://www.camh.ca

Dougy Center
https://www.dougy.org

Drug Free Kids Canada (DFKC)
https://www.drugfreekidscanada.org

The Grief Toolbox
https://thegrieftoolbox.com

Hope for Wellness Helpline
https://www.hopeforwellness.ca

Kids Help Phone
https://kidshelpphone.ca

The Mood Disorders Society of Canada (MDSC)
https://mdsc.ca

Narcotics Anonymous (NA)
https://na.org

  ISBN: 978-1-77492-094-7